SILLY NOVELS

BY LADY NOVELISTS

AND OTHER ESSAYS

Silly Novels by Lady Novelists
and other essays

GEORGE ELIOT
MARY ANN EVANS

RENARD PRESS

RENARD PRESS LTD

124 City Road
London EC1V 2NX
United Kingdom
info@renardpress.com
020 8050 2928

www.renardpress.com

'Silly Novels by Lady Novelists' first published in 1856; 'Woman in France' first published in 1854; 'The Grammar of Ornament' first published in 1865; 'The Too-Ready Writer' and 'Diseases of Small Authorship' first published in 1879. For more information on first publications see Notes on p. 103.
This selection first published by Renard Press Ltd in 2023

Edited text, selection and Notes © Renard Press Ltd, 2023

Cover design by Will Dady

Printed and bound in the UK on carbon-balanced papers by CMP Books

ISBN: 978-1-80447-033-6

9 8 7 6 5 4 3

CLIMATE POSITIVE Renard Press is proud to be a climate positive publisher, removing more carbon from the air than we emit and planting a small forest. For more information see renardpress.com/eco.

All rights reserved. This publication may not be reproduced, stored in a retrieval system or transmitted, in any form or by any means – electronic, mechanical, photocopying, recording or otherwise – without the prior permission of the publisher.

EU Authorised Representative: Easy Access System Europe
Mustamäe tee 50, 10621 Tallinn, Estonia
gpsr.requests@easproject.com.

CONTENTS

Silly Novels by Lady Novelists and Other Essays	1
Silly Novels by Lady Novelists	3
Woman in France	37
The Grammar of Ornament	77
The Too-Ready Writer	81
Diseases of Small Authorship	91
Notes	103

SILLY NOVELS

BY LADY NOVELISTS

AND OTHER ESSAYS

SILLY NOVELS

BY LADY NOVELISTS

SILLY NOVELS BY LADY NOVELISTS are a genus with many species, determined by the particular quality of silliness that predominates in them – the frothy, the prosy, the pious or the pedantic. But it is a mixture of all these – a composite order of feminine fatuity – that produces the largest class of such novels, which we shall distinguish as the *mind-and-millinery* species. The heroine is usually an heiress, probably a peeress in her own right, with perhaps a vicious baronet, an amiable duke and an irresistible younger son of a marquis as lovers in the foreground, a clergyman and a poet sighing for her in the middle distance and a crowd of undefined adorers dimly indicated beyond. Her eyes and her wit are both dazzling; her nose and her morals are alike free from any tendency to irregularity; she has a superb contralto and a superb intellect; she is perfectly well dressed and perfectly religious; she dances like a sylph and reads the Bible in the original tongues. Or it may be that the heroine is not an heiress – that rank and wealth are the only things in which she is deficient; but she infallibly gets into high society, she has the triumph of refusing many matches and securing the best, and she wears some family jewels or other as a sort of crown of righteousness at the end. Rakish men either bite their lips in impotent confusion at her repartees, or are touched to penitence by her reproofs, which, on appropriate occasions, rise to a lofty strain of rhetoric; indeed, there is a general propensity in her to make speeches, and to rhapsodise at some length when she retires to her bedroom. In her recorded conversations she is amazingly eloquent, and in her unrecorded conversations amazingly witty. She is understood to have a depth of insight that looks through and through the shallow theories of philosophers, and her superior instincts are a sort of dial by which men have only to set their clocks and watches, and all will go well. The men play a very subordinate part by her side. You are consoled now and then by a hint that they have affairs, which keeps you in mind that the working-day business of the world is somehow being carried on, but ostensibly the final cause of their existence is that they may accompany the heroine on her 'starring' expedition through life. They see her at a ball, and they are dazzled; at a flower show, and they are fascinated; on a riding excursion, and they are witched by her noble horsemanship; at church, and they are awed by the sweet solemnity of her demeanour. She is the ideal woman in feelings, faculties and flounces. For all this she as often as not marries the wrong person to begin with, and she suffers terribly from the plots and intrigues of the vicious baronet; but even death has a soft place in his heart for such a paragon, and remedies all mistakes for her just at the right moment. The vicious baronet is sure to be killed in a duel, and the tedious husband dies in his bed requesting his wife, as a particular favour to him, to marry the man she loves best, and having already dispatched a note to the lover informing him of the comfortable arrangement. Before matters arrive at this desirable issue our feelings are tried by seeing the noble, lovely and gifted heroine pass through many *mauvais moments*,* but we have the satisfaction of knowing that her sorrows are wept into embroidered pocket handkerchiefs, that her fainting form reclines on the very best upholstery, and that whatever vicissitudes she may undergo, from being dashed out of her carriage to having her head shaved in a fever, she comes out of them all with a complexion more blooming and locks more redundant than ever.

We may remark, by the way, that we have been relieved from a serious scruple by discovering that silly novels by lady novelists rarely introduce us into any other than very lofty and fashionable society. We had imagined that destitute women turned novelists, as they turned governesses, because they had no other 'ladylike' means of getting their bread. On this supposition, vacillating syntax and improbable incident had a certain pathos for us, like the extremely supererogatory pincushions and ill-devised nightcaps that are offered for sale by a blind man. We felt the commodity to be a nuisance, but we were glad to think that the money went to relieve the necessitous, and we pictured to ourselves lonely women struggling for a maintenance, or wives and daughters devoting themselves to the production of 'copy' out of pure heroism – perhaps to pay their husband's debts or to purchase luxuries for a sick father. Under these impressions we shrank from criticising a lady's novel: her English might be faulty, but we said to ourselves her motives are irreproachable; her imagination may be uninventive, but her patience is untiring. Empty writing was excused by an empty stomach, and twaddle was consecrated by tears. But no! This theory of ours, like many other pretty theories, has had to give way before observation. Women's silly novels, we are now convinced, are written under totally different circumstances. The fair writers have evidently never talked to a tradesman except from a carriage window; they have no notion of the working classes except as 'dependents'; they think five hundred a year a miserable pittance; Belgravia and 'baronial halls' are their primary truths; and they have no idea of feeling interest in any man who is not at least a great landed proprietor, if not a prime minister. It is clear that they write in elegant boudoirs, with violet-coloured ink and a ruby pen; that they must be entirely indifferent to publishers' accounts, and inexperienced in every form of poverty except poverty of brains. It is true that we are constantly struck with the want of verisimilitude in their representations of the high society in which they seem to live; but then they betray no closer acquaintance with any other form of life. If their peers and peeresses are improbable, their literary men, tradespeople and cottagers are impossible; and their intellect seems to have the peculiar impartiality of reproducing both what they have seen and heard, and what they have not seen and heard, with equal unfaithfulness.

There are few women, we suppose, who have not seen something of children under five years of age, yet in Compensation, a recent novel of the mind-and-millinery species, which calls itself a 'story of real life',* we have a child of four-and-a-half years old talking in this Ossianic* fashion:

'Oh, I am so happy, dear Grandmamma; I have seen – I have seen such a delightful person; he is like everything beautiful – like the smell of sweet flowers, and the view from Ben Lemond – or no, *better than that* – he is like what I think of and see when I am very, very happy; and he is really like Mamma, too, when she sings; and his forehead is like *that distant sea*,' she continued, pointing to the blue Mediterranean; 'there seems no end – no end; or like the clusters of stars I like best to look at on a warm fine night... Don't look so... your forehead is like Loch Lomond, when the wind is blowing and the sun is gone in; I like the sunshine best when the lake is smooth... So now – I like it better than ever... It is more beautiful still from the dark cloud that has gone over it, *when the sun suddenly lights up all the colours of the forests and shining purple rocks, and it is all reflected in the waters below.*'

We are not surprised to learn that the mother of this infant phenomenon, who exhibits symptoms so alarmingly like those of adolescence repressed by gin, is herself a phoenix. We are assured, again and again, that she had a remarkably original mind, that she was a genius and 'conscious of her originality', and she was fortunate enough to have a lover who was also a genius and a man of 'most original mind'.

This lover, we read, though 'wonderfully similar' to her 'in powers and capacity', was 'infinitely superior to her in faith and development', and she saw in him '"Agape"* – so rare to find – of which she had read and admired the meaning in her Greek Testament; having, *from her great facility in learning languages*, read the Scriptures in their original *tongues.*' Of course! Greek and Hebrew are mere play to a heroine;

Sanskrit is no more than *a b c* to her; and she can talk with perfect correctness in any language, except English. She is a polking polyglot, a Creuzer* in crinoline. Poor men. There are so few of you who know even Hebrew; you think it something to boast of if, like Bolingbroke, you only 'understand that sort of learning and what is writ about it',* and you are perhaps adoring women who can think slightingly of you in all the Semitic languages successively. But then, as we are almost invariably told that a heroine has a 'beautifully small head', and as her intellect has probably been early invigorated by an attention to costume and deportment, we may conclude that she can pick up the Oriental tongues, to say nothing of their dialects, with the same aerial facility that the butterfly sips nectar. Besides, there can be no difficulty in conceiving the depth of the heroine's erudition when that of the authoress is so evident.

In *Laura Gay*,* another novel of the same school, the heroine seems less at home in Greek and Hebrew, but she makes up for the deficiency by a quite playful familiarity with the Latin classics – with the 'dear old Virgil', 'the graceful Horace, the humane Cicero and the pleasant Livy';* indeed, it is such a matter of course with her to quote Latin that she does it at a picnic in a very mixed company of ladies and gentlemen, having, we are told, 'no conception that the nobler sex were capable of jealousy on this subject. And if, indeed,' continues the biographer of Laura Gray, 'the wisest and noblest portion of that sex were in the majority, no such sentiment would exist; but while Miss Wyndhams and Mr Redfords abound, great sacrifices must be made to their existence.' Such sacrifices, we presume, as abstaining from Latin quotations, of extremely moderate interest and applicability, which the wise and noble minority of the other sex would be quite as willing to dispense with as the foolish and ignoble majority. It is as little the custom of well-bred men as of well-bred women to quote Latin in mixed parties; they can contain their familiarity with 'the humane Cicero' without allowing it to boil over in ordinary conversation, and even references to 'the pleasant Livy' are not absolutely irrepressible. But Ciceronian Latin is the mildest form of Miss Gay's conversational power. Being on the Palatine with a party of sightseers, she falls into the following vein of well-rounded remark:

> Truth can only be pure objectively, for even in the creeds where it predominates, being subjective, and parcelled out into portions, each of these necessarily receives a hue of idiosyncrasy – that is, a taint of superstition more or less strong; while in such creeds as the Roman Catholic, ignorance, interest, the basis of ancient idolatries and the force of authority, have gradually accumulated on the pure truth, and transformed it, at last, into a mass of superstition for the majority of its votaries; and how few are there, alas! whose zeal, courage and intellectual energy are equal to the analysis of this accumulation, and to the discovery of the pearl of great price which lies hidden beneath this heap of rubbish.

We have often met with women much more novel and profound in their observations than Laura Gay, but rarely with any so inopportunely long-winded. A clerical lord, who is half in love with her, is alarmed by the daring remarks just quoted, and begins to suspect that she is inclined to free-thinking. But he is mistaken; when in a moment of sorrow he delicately begs leave to 'recall to her memory, a *depôt** of strength and consolation under affliction, which, until we are hard pressed by the trials of life, we are too apt to forget,' we learn that she really has 'recurrence to that sacred *depôt*', together with the teapot. There is a certain flavour of orthodoxy mixed with the parade of fortunes and fine carriages in *Laura Gay*, but it is an orthodoxy mitigated by study of 'the humane Cicero', and by an 'intellectual disposition to analyse'.

Compensation is much more heavily dosed with doctrine, but then it has a treble amount of snobbish worldliness and absurd incident to tickle the palate of pious frivolity. Linda, the heroine, is still more speculative and spiritual than Laura Gay, but she has been 'presented', and has more and far grander lovers; very wicked and fascinating women are introduced – even a French *lionne*;* and no expense is spared to get up as exciting a story as you will find in the most immoral novels. In fact, it is a wonderful potpourri of Almack's,* Scotch second sight, Mr Rogers's breakfasts,* Italian brigands, deathbed conversions, superior authoresses, Italian mistresses and attempts at poisoning old ladies, the whole served up with a garnish of talk about 'faith and development' and 'most original minds'. Even Miss Susan Barton, the superior authoress, whose pen moves in a 'quick, decided manner when she is composing', declines the finest opportunities of marriage; and though old enough to be Linda's mother (since we are told that she refused Linda's father), has her hand sought by a young earl, the heroine's rejected lover. Of course, genius and morality must be backed by eligible offers, or they would seem rather a dull affair; and piety, like other things, in order to be *comme il faut*,* must be in 'society', and have admittance to the best circles.

*Rank and Beauty** is a more frothy and less religious variety of the mind-and-millinery species. The heroine, we are told, 'if she inherited her father's pride of birth and her mother's beauty of person, had in herself a tone of enthusiastic feeling that, perhaps, belongs to her age even in the lowly born, but which is refined into the high spirit of wild romance only in the far descended, who feel that it is their best inheritance.' This enthusiastic young lady, by dint of reading the newspaper to her father, falls in love with the *prime minister*, who, through the medium of leading articles and 'the *resumé* of the debates,' shines upon her imagination as a bright particular star, which has no parallax for her living in the country as simple Miss Wyndham. But she forthwith becomes Baroness Umfraville in her own right, astonishes the world with her beauty and accomplishments when she bursts upon it from her mansion in Spring Gardens,* and, as you foresee, will presently come into contact with the unseen *objet aimé*.* Perhaps the words 'prime minister' suggest to you a wrinkled or obese sexagenarian; but pray dismiss the image. Lord Rupert Conway has been 'called while still almost a youth to the first situation which a subject can hold in the *universe*', and even leading articles and a *resumé* of the debates have not conjured up a dream that surpasses the fact.

> The door opened again, and Lord Rupert Conway entered. Evelyn gave one glance. It was enough; she was not disappointed. It seemed as if a picture on which she

had long gazed was suddenly instinct with life, and had stepped from its frame before her. His tall figure, the distinguished simplicity of his air – it was a living Vandyke,* a cavalier, one of his noble cavalier ancestors, or one to whom her fancy had always likened him, who long of yore had with an Umfraville fought the Paynim far beyond the sea. Was this reality?

Very little like it, certainly.

By and by it becomes evident that the ministerial heart is touched. Lady Umfraville is on a visit to the Queen at Windsor, and:

> The last evening of her stay, when they returned from riding, Mr Wyndham took her and a large party to the top of the keep, to see the view. She was leaning on the battlements, gazing from that 'stately height' at the prospect beneath her, when Lord Rupert was by her side. 'What an unrivalled view!' exclaimed she.
>
> 'Yes, it would have been wrong to go without having been up here. You are pleased with your visit?'
>
> 'Enchanted! A queen to live and die under, to live and die for!'
>
> 'Ha!' cried he, with sudden emotion, and with a *eureka* expression of countenance, as if he had *indeed found a heart in unison with his own*.

The '*eureka* expression of countenance' you see at once to be prophetic of marriage at the end of the third volume; but before that desirable consummation there are very complicated misunderstandings, arising chiefly from the vindictive plotting of Sir Luttrel Wycherley, who is a genius, a poet and in every way a most remarkable character indeed. He is not only a romantic poet, but a hardened rake and a cynical wit; yet his deep passion for Lady Umfraville has so impoverished his epigrammatic talent that he cuts an extremely poor figure in conversation. When she rejects him, he rushes into the shrubbery and rolls himself in the dirt; and on recovering, devotes himself to the most diabolical and laborious schemes of vengeance, in the course of which he disguises himself as a quack physician and enters into general practice, foreseeing that Evelyn will fall ill, and that he shall be called in to attend her. At last, when all his schemes are frustrated, he takes leave of her in a long letter, written, as you will perceive from the following passage, entirely in the style of an eminent literary man:

> Oh, lady, nursed in pomp and pleasure, will you ever cast one thought upon the miserable being who addresses you? Will you ever, as your gilded galley is floating down the unruffled stream of prosperity, will you ever, while lulled by the sweetest music – thine own praises – hear the far-off sigh from that world to which I am going?

On the whole, however, frothy as it is, we rather prefer *Rank and Beauty* to the two other novels we have mentioned. The dialogue is more natural and spirited; there is some frank ignorance and no pedantry; and you are allowed to take the heroine's astounding intellect upon trust, without being called on to read her conversational refutations of sceptics and philosophers, or her rhetorical solutions of the mysteries of the universe.

Writers of the mind-and-millinery school are remarkably unanimous in their choice of diction. In their novels there is usually a lady or gentleman who is more or less of a upas tree:* the lover has a manly breast; minds are redolent of various things; hearts are hollow; events are utilised; friends are consigned to the tomb; infancy is an engaging period; the sun is a luminary that goes to his western couch, or gathers the raindrops into his refulgent bosom; life is a melancholy boon; Albion and Scotia are conversational epithets. There is a striking resemblance, too, in the character of their moral comments – such, for instance, as that 'It is a fact, no less true than melancholy, that all people, more or less, richer or poorer, are swayed by bad example';* that 'Books, however trivial, contain some subjects from which useful information may be drawn'; that 'Vice can too often borrow the language of virtue'; that 'Merit and nobility of nature must exist, to be accepted, for clamour and pretension cannot impose upon those too well read in human nature to be easily deceived'; and that 'In order to forgive, we must have been injured'. There is doubtless a class of readers to whom these remarks appear peculiarly pointed and pungent; for we often find them doubly and trebly scored with the pencil, and delicate hands giving in their determined adhesion to these hardy novelties by a distinct *très vrai*,* emphasised by many notes of exclamation. The colloquial style of these novels is often marked by much ingenious inversion, and a careful avoidance of such cheap phraseology as can be heard every day. Angry young gentlemen exclaim, ''Tis ever thus, methinks'; and in the half hour before dinner a young lady informs her next neighbour that the first day she read Shakespeare she 'stole away into the park, and, beneath the shadow of the greenwood tree, devoured with rapture the inspired page of the great magician.' But the most remarkable efforts of the mind-and-millinery writers lie in their philosophic reflections. The authoress of *Laura Gay*, for example, having married her hero and heroine, improves the event by observing that, 'if those sceptics, whose eyes have so long gazed on matter that they can no longer see aught else in man, could once enter with heart and soul, into such bliss as this, they would come to say that the soul of man and the polypus are not of common origin, or of the same texture.' Lady novelists, it appears, can see something else besides matter; they are not limited to phenomena, but can relieve their eyesight by occasional glimpses of the *noumenon*,* and are, therefore, naturally better able than anyone else to confound sceptics, even of that remarkable but to us unknown school which maintains that the soul of man is of the same texture as the polypus.

The most pitiable of all silly novels by lady novelists are what we may call the *oracular* species – novels intended to expound the writer's religious, philosophical or moral theories. There seems to be a notion abroad among women, rather akin to the superstition that the speech and actions of idiots are inspired, and that the human being most entirely exhausted of common sense is the fittest vehicle of revelation. To judge from their writings, there are certain ladies who think that an amazing ignorance, both of science and of life, is the best possible qualification for forming an opinion on the knottiest moral and speculative questions. Apparently their recipe for solving all such difficulties is something like this: take a woman's head, stuff it with a smattering of philosophy and literature chopped small, and with false notions of society baked hard, let it hang over a desk a few hours every day, and serve up hot in feeble English when not required. You will rarely meet with a lady novelist of the oracular class who is diffident of her ability to decide on theological questions – who has any suspicion that she is not capable of discriminating with the nicest accuracy between the good and evil in all church parties – who does not see precisely how it is that men have gone wrong hitherto – and pity philosophers in general that they have not had the opportunity of consulting her. Great writers, who have modestly contented themselves with putting their experience into fiction, and have thought it quite a sufficient task to exhibit men and things as they are, she sighs over as deplorably deficient in the application of their powers. 'They have solved no great questions' – and she is ready to remedy their omission by setting before you a complete theory of life and manual of divinity in a love story, where ladies and gentlemen of good family go through genteel vicissitudes, to the utter confusion of Deists, Puseyites* and ultra-Protestants, and to the perfect establishment of that peculiar view of Christianity which either condenses itself into a sentence of small caps, or explodes into a cluster of stars on the three hundred and thirtieth page. It is true, the ladies and gentlemen will probably seem to you remarkably little like any you have had the fortune or misfortune to meet with, for, as a general rule, the ability of a lady novelist to describe actual life and her fellow men is in inverse proportion to her confident eloquence about God and the other world, and the means by which she usually chooses to conduct you to true ideas of the invisible is a totally false picture of the visible.

SILLY NOVELS BY LADY NOVELISTS

As typical a novel of the oracular kind as we can hope to meet with, is *The Enigma: A Leaf from the Chronicles of the Wolchorley House.** The 'enigma' which this novel is to solve is certainly one that demands powers no less gigantic than those of a lady novelist, being neither more nor less than the existence of evil. The problem is stated and the answer dimly foreshadowed on the very first page. The spirited young lady, with raven hair, says, 'All life is an inextricable confusion'; and the meek young lady, with auburn hair, looks at the picture of the Madonna which she is copying, and – '*There* seemed the solution of that mighty enigma.' The style of this novel is quite as lofty as its purpose; indeed, some passages on which we have spent much patient study are quite beyond our reach, in spite of the illustrative aid of italics and small caps; and we must await further 'development' in order to understand them. Of Ernest, the model young clergyman, who sets everyone right on all occasions, we read that 'he held not of marriage in the marketable kind, after a social desecration'; that, on one eventful night, 'sleep had not visited his divided heart, where tumultuated, in varied type and combination, the aggregate feelings of grief and joy'; and that, 'for the *marketable* human article he had no toleration, be it of what sort, or set for what value it might, whether for worship or class, his upright soul abhorred it, whose ultimatum, the self-deceiver, was to him THE *great spiritual lie*, "living in a vain show, deceiving and being deceived"; since he did not suppose the phylactery and enlarged border on the garment to be *merely* a social trick.' (The italics and small caps are the author's, and we hope they assist the reader's comprehension.) Of Sir Lionel, the model old gentleman, we are told that 'the simple ideal of the middle age, apart from its anarchy and decadence, in him most truly seemed to live again, when the ties which knit men together were of heroic cast. The first-born colours of pristine faith and truth engraven on the common soul of man, and blent into the wide arch of brotherhood, where the primeval law of *order* grew and multiplied each perfect after his kind, and mutually interdependent.' You see clearly, of course, how colours are first engraven on the soul, and then blent into a wide arch, on which arch of colours – apparently a rainbow – the law of order grew and multiplied, each – apparently the arch and the law – perfect after his kind? If, after this, you can possibly want any further aid towards knowing what Sir Lionel was, we can tell you that in his soul 'the scientific combinations of thought could educe no fuller harmonies of the good and the true than lay in the primeval pulses which floated as an atmosphere around it!' and that, when he was sealing a letter, 'Lo! the responsive throb in that good man's bosom echoed back in simple truth the honest witness of a heart that condemned him not, as his eye, bedewed with love, rested, too, with something of ancestral pride, on the undimmed motto of the family – "LOIAUTÉ".'*

The slightest matters have their vulgarity fumigated out of them by the same elevated style. Commonplace people would say that a copy of Shakespeare lay on a drawing-room table; but the authoress of *The Enigma*, bent on edifying periphrasis, tells you that there lay on the table 'that fund of human thought and feeling, which teaches the heart through the little name, "Shakespeare"'. A watchman sees a light burning in an upper window rather longer than usual, and thinks that people are foolish to sit up late when they have an opportunity of going to bed; but, lest this fact should seem too low and common, it is presented to us in the following striking and metaphysical manner: 'He marvelled – as a man *will* think for others in a necessarily separate personality, consequently (though disallowing it) in false mental premise – how differently *he* should act, how gladly *he* should prize the rest so lightly held of within.' A footman – an ordinary Jeames, with large calves and aspirated vowels – answers the doorbell, and the opportunity is seized to tell you that he was a 'type of the large class of pampered menials, who follow the curse of Cain – "vagabonds" on the face of the earth, and whose estimate of the human class varies in the graduated scale of money and expenditure... These, and such as these, O England, be the false lights of thy morbid civilisation!' We have heard of various 'false lights', from Dr Cumming to Robert Owen, from Dr Pusey* to the spirit-rappers,* but we never before heard of the false light that emanates from plush and powder.

In the same way very ordinary events of civilised life are exalted into the most awful crises, and ladies in full skirts and *manches à la chinoise** conduct themselves not unlike the heroines of sanguinary melodramas. Mrs Percy, a shallow woman of the world, wishes her son Horace to marry the auburn-haired Grace, she being an heiress; but he, after the manner of sons, falls in love with the raven-haired Kate, the heiress's portionless cousin; and, moreover, Grace herself shows every symptom of perfect indifference to Horace. In such cases sons are often sulky or fiery, mothers are alternately manoeuvring and waspish, and the portionless young lady often lies awake at night and cries a good deal. We are getting used to these things now, just as we are used to eclipses of the moon, which no longer set us howling and beating tin kettles.

We never heard of a lady in a fashionable 'front' behaving like Mrs Percy under these circumstances. Happening one day to see Horace talking to Grace at a window, without in the least knowing what they are talking about, or having the least reason to believe that Grace, who is mistress of the house and a person of dignity, would accept her son if he were to offer himself, she suddenly rushes up to them and clasps them both, saying, 'with a flushed countenance and in an excited manner' – 'This is indeed happiness; for, may I not call you so, Grace? – my Grace – my Horace's Grace! – my dear children!' Her son tells her she is mistaken, and that he is engaged to Kate, whereupon we have the following scene and tableau:

> Gathering herself up to an unprecedented height,(!) her eyes lightening forth the fire of her anger:
> 'Wretched boy!' she said, hoarsely and scornfully, and clenching her hand, 'Take then the doom of your own choice! Bow down your miserable head and let a mother's—'
> 'Curse not!' spake a deep low voice from behind, and Mrs Percy started, scared, as though she had seen a heavenly visitant appear, to break upon her in the midst of her sin.
> Meantime, Horace had fallen on his knees, at her feet, and hid his face in his hands.
> 'Who, then, is she – who! Truly his 'guardian spirit' hath stepped between him and the fearful words, which, however unmerited, must have hung as a pall over his future existence; a spell which could not be unbound – which could not be unsaid.

Of an earthly paleness, but calm with the still, iron-bound calmness of death – the only calm one there – Katherine stood; and her words smote on the ear in tones whose appallingly slow and separate intonation rung on the heart like a chill, isolated tolling of some fatal knell.

'He would have plighted me his faith, but I did not accept it; you cannot, therefore – you *dare* not curse him. And here,' she continued, raising her hand to heaven, whither her large, dark eyes also rose with a chastened glow, which, for the first time, *suffering* had lighted in those passionate orbs – 'here I promise, come weal, come woe, that Horace Wolchorley and I do never interchange vows without his mother's sanction – without his mother's blessing!'

Here, and throughout the story, we see that confusion of purpose which is so characteristic of silly novels written by women. It is a story of quite modern drawing-room society – a society in which polkas are played and Puseyism discussed; yet we have characters, and incidents, and traits of manner introduced, which are mere shreds from the most heterogeneous romances. We have a blind Irish harper, 'relic of the picturesque bards of yore', startling us at a Sunday-school festival of tea and cake in an English village; we have a crazy gypsy, in a scarlet cloak, singing snatches of romantic song, and revealing a secret on her deathbed which, with the testimony of a dwarfish miserly merchant, who salutes strangers with a curse and a devilish laugh, goes to prove that Ernest, the model young clergyman, is Kate's brother; and we have an ultra-virtuous Irish Barney discovering that a document is forged, by comparing the date of the paper with the date of the alleged signature, although the same document has passed through a court of law and occasioned a fatal decision. The 'Hall' in which Sir Lionel lives is the venerable country seat of an old family, and this, we suppose, sets the imagination of the authoress flying to donjons and battlements, where 'lo! the warder blows his horn'; for, as the inhabitants are in their bedrooms on a night certainly within the recollection of Pleaceman X,* and a breeze springs up, which we are at first told was faint, and then that it made the old cedars bow their branches to the greensward, she falls into this medieval vein of description (the italics are ours):

> The banner *unfurled it* at the sound, and shook its guardian wing above, while the startled owl *flapped her* in the ivy; the firmament looking down through her 'argus eyes' –
> Ministers of heaven's mute melodies.
> And lo! two strokes tolled from out the warder tower, and 'Two o'clock' re-echoed its interpreter below.

Such stories as this of *The Enigma* remind us of the pictures clever children sometimes draw 'out of their own head', where you will see a modern villa on the right, two knights in helmets fighting in the foreground and a tiger grinning in a jungle on the left, the several objects being brought together because the artist thinks each pretty, and perhaps still more because he remembers seeing them in other pictures.

But we like the authoress much better on her medieval stilts than on her oracular ones – when she talks of the *Ich* and of 'subjective' and 'objective', and lays down the exact line of Christian verity, between 'right-hand excesses and left-hand declensions'. Persons who deviate from this line are introduced with a patronising air of charity. Of a certain

Miss Inshquine she informs us, with all the lucidity of italics and small caps, that '*function*, not *form*, AS THE INEVITABLE OUTER EXPRESSION OF THE SPIRIT IN THIS TABERNACLE AGE, weakly engrossed her'. And apropos of Miss Mayjar, an evangelical lady who is a little too apt to talk of her visits to sick women and the state of their souls, we are told that the model clergyman is 'not one to disallow, through the *super* crust, the undercurrent towards good in the *subject*, or the positive benefits, nevertheless, to the *object*'. We imagine the double-refined accent and protrusion of chin which are feebly represented by the italics in this lady's sentences! We abstain from quoting any of her oracular doctrinal passages, because they refer to matters too serious for our pages just now.

The epithet 'silly' may seem impertinent, applied to a novel which indicates so much reading and intellectual activity as *The Enigma*, but we use this epithet advisedly. If, as the world has long agreed, a very great amount of instruction will not make a wise man, still less will a very mediocre amount of instruction make a wise woman. And the most mischievous form of feminine silliness is the literary form, because it tends to confirm the popular prejudice against the more solid education of women.

When men see girls wasting their time in consultations about bonnets and ball dresses, and in giggling or sentimental love confidences, or middle-aged women mismanaging their children and solacing themselves with acrid gossip, they can hardly help saying, 'For Heaven's sake, let girls be better educated; let them have some better objects of thought – some more solid occupations.' But after a few hours' conversation with an oracular literary woman, or a few hours' reading of her books, they are likely enough to say, 'After all, when a woman gets some knowledge, see what use she makes of it! Her knowledge remains acquisition instead of passing into culture; instead of being subdued into modesty and simplicity by a larger acquaintance with thought and fact, she has a feverish consciousness of her attainments; she keeps a sort of mental pocket mirror, and is continually looking in it at her own "intellectuality"; she spoils the taste of one's muffin by questions of metaphysics; "puts down" men at a dinner table with her superior information; and seizes the opportunity of a soirée to catechise us on the vital question of the relation between mind and matter. And then, look at her writings! She mistakes vagueness for depth, bombast for eloquence and affectation for originality; she struts on one page, rolls her eyes on another, grimaces in a third and is hysterical in a fourth. She may have read many writings of great men, and a few writings of great women; but she is as unable to discern the difference between her own style and theirs as a Yorkshireman is to discern the difference between his own English and a Londoner's: rodomontade is the native accent of her intellect. No – the average nature of women is too shallow and feeble a soil to bear much tillage; it is only fit for the very lightest crops.'

It is true that the men who come to such a decision on such very superficial and imperfect observation may not be among the wisest in the world; but we have not now to contest their opinion – we are only pointing out how it is unconsciously encouraged by many women who have volunteered themselves as representatives of the feminine intellect. We do not believe that a man was ever strengthened in such an opinion by associating with a woman of true culture, whose mind had absorbed her knowledge instead of being absorbed by it. A really cultured woman, like a really cultured man, is all the simpler and the less obtrusive for her knowledge; it has made her see herself and her opinions in something like just proportions; she does not make it a pedestal from which she flatters herself that she commands a complete view of men and things, but makes it a point of observation from which to form a right estimate of herself. She neither spouts poetry nor quotes Cicero on slight provocation; not because she thinks that a sacrifice must be made to the prejudices of men, but because that mode of exhibiting her memory and Latinity does not present itself to her as edifying or graceful. She does not write books to confound philosophers, perhaps because she is able to write books that delight them. In conversation she is the least formidable of women, because she understands you, without wanting to make you aware that you *can't* understand her. She does not give you information, which is the raw material of culture – she gives you sympathy, which is its subtlest essence.

A more numerous class of silly novels than the oracular (which are generally inspired by some form of High Church or transcendental Christianity) is what we may call the *white neckcloth* species, which represent the tone of thought and feeling in the Evangelical party. This species is a kind of genteel tract on a large scale, intended as a sort of medicinal sweetmeat for Low Church young ladies; an Evangelical substitute for the fashionable novel, as the May Meetings* are a substitute for the Opera. Even Quaker children, one would think, can hardly have been denied the indulgence of a doll; but it must be a doll dressed in a drab gown and a coal-scuttle bonnet – not a worldly doll, in gauze and spangles. And there are no young ladies, we imagine – unless they belong to the Church of the United Brethren,* in which people are married without any lovemaking – who can dispense with love stories. Thus, for Evangelical young ladies there are Evangelical love stories, in which the vicissitudes of the tender passion are sanctified by saving views of Regeneration and the Atonement. These novels differ from the oracular ones, as a Low Churchwoman often differs from a High Churchwoman: they are a little less supercilious and a great deal more ignorant, a little less correct in their syntax and a great deal more vulgar.

The Orlando* of Evangelical literature is the young curate, looked at from the point of view of the middle class, where cambric bands are understood to have as thrilling an effect on the hearts of young ladies as epaulettes have in the classes above and below it. In the ordinary type of these novels the hero is almost sure to be a young curate, frowned upon, perhaps, by worldly mammas, but carrying captive the hearts of their daughters, who can 'never forget *that* sermon'; tender glances are seized from the pulpit stairs instead of the opera box; tête-à-têtes are seasoned with quotations from Scripture instead of quotations from the poets; and questions as to the state of the heroine's affections are mingled with anxieties as to the state of her soul. The young curate always has a background of well-dressed and wealthy if not fashionable society – for Evangelical silliness is as snobbish as any other kind of silliness – and the Evangelical lady novelist, while she explains to you the type of the scapegoat on one page, is ambitious on another to represent the manners and conversations of aristocratic people. Her pictures of fashionable society are often curious studies, considered as efforts of the Evangelical imagination; but in one particular the novels of the White Neckcloth School are meritoriously realistic – their favourite hero, the Evangelical young curate, is always rather an insipid personage.

The most recent novel of this species that we happen to have before us is *The Old Grey Church*.* It is utterly tame and feeble; there is no one set of objects on which the writer seems to have a stronger grasp than on any other; and we should be entirely at a loss to conjecture among what phases of life her experience has been gained, but for certain vulgarisms of style which sufficiently indicate that she has had the advantage, though she has been unable to use it, of mingling chiefly with men and women whose manners and characters have not had all their bosses and angles rubbed down by refined conventionalism. It is less excusable in an Evangelical novelist, than in any other, gratuitously to seek her subjects among titles and carriages. The real drama of Evangelicalism – and it has abundance of fine drama for anyone who has genius enough to discern and reproduce it – lies among the middle and lower classes; and are not Evangelical opinions understood to give an especial interest in the weak things of the earth, rather than in the mighty? Why, then, cannot our Evangelical lady novelists show us the operation of their religious views among people (there really are many such in the world) who keep no carriage, 'not so much as a brass-bound gig', who even manage to eat their dinner without a silver fork, and in whose mouths the authoress's questionable English would be strictly consistent? Why can we not have pictures of religious life among the industrial classes in England, as interesting as Mrs Stowe's pictures of religious life among the Negroes?* Instead of this pious ladies nauseate us with novels which remind us of what we sometimes see in a worldly woman recently 'converted' – she is as fond of a fine dinner table as before, but she invites clergymen instead of beaux; she thinks as much of her dress as before, but she adopts a more sober choice of colours and patterns; her conversation is as trivial as before, but the triviality is flavoured with gospel instead of gossip. In *The Old Grey Church* we have the same sort of Evangelical travesty of the fashionable novel, and of course the vicious, intriguing baronet is not wanting. It is worthwhile to give a sample of the style of conversation attributed to this high-born rake – a style that, in its profuse italics and palpable innuendoes, is worthy of Miss Squeers.* In an evening visit to the ruins of the Colosseum, Eustace, the young clergyman, has been withdrawing the heroine, Miss Lushington, from the rest of the party, for the sake of a tête-à-tête. The baronet is jealous, and vents his pique in this way:

> There they are, and Miss Lushington, no doubt, quite safe; for she is under the holy guidance of Pope Eustace the First, who has, of course, been delivering to her an edifying homily on the wickedness of the heathens of yore, who, as tradition tells us, in this very place let loose the wild *beasties* on poor St Paul! Oh, no! by the by, I believe I am wrong, and betraying my want of clergy, and that it was not at all St Paul, nor was it here. But no matter, it would equally serve as a text to preach from, and from which to diverge to the degenerate *heathen* Christians of the present day, and all their naughty practices, and so end with an exhortation to 'come but from among them, and be separate' – and I am sure, Miss Lushington, you

have most scrupulously conformed to that injunction this evening, for we have seen nothing of you since our arrival. But everyone seems agreed it has been a *charming party of pleasure*, and I am sure we all feel *much indebted* to Mr Grey for having *suggested* it; and as he seems so capital a cicerone, I hope he will think of something else equally agreeable to *all*.

This drivelling kind of dialogue, and equally drivelling narrative, which, like a bad drawing, represents nothing, and barely indicates what is meant to be represented, runs through the book; and we have no doubt is considered by the amiable authoress to constitute an improving novel, which Christian mothers will do well to put into the hands of their daughters. But everything is relative; we have met with American vegetarians whose normal diet was dry meal, and who, when their appetite wanted stimulating, tickled it with *wet* meal; and so, we can imagine that there are Evangelical circles in which *The Old Grey Church* is devoured as a powerful and interesting fiction.

But perhaps the least readable of silly women's novels are the *modern-antique* species, which unfold to us the domestic life of Jannes and Jambres, the private love affairs of Sennacherib or the mental struggles and ultimate conversion of Demetrius the silversmith.* From most silly novels we can at least extract a laugh; but those of the modern-antique school have a ponderous, a leaden kind of fatuity, under which we groan. What can be more demonstrative of the inability of literary women to measure their own powers than their frequent assumption of a task which can only be justified by the rarest concurrence of acquirement with genius? The finest effort to reanimate the past is of course only approximative — is always more or less an infusion of the modern spirit into the ancient form:

> *Was ihr den Geist der Zeiten heisst,*
> *Das ist im Grund der Herren eigner Geist,*
> *In dem die Zeiten sich bespiegeln.**

Admitting that genius which has familiarised itself with all the relics of an ancient period can sometimes, by the force of its sympathetic divination, restore the missing notes in the 'music of humanity', and reconstruct the fragments into a whole which will really bring the remote past nearer to us, and interpret it to our duller apprehension — this form of imaginative power must always be among the very rarest, because it demands as much accurate and minute knowledge as creative vigour. Yet we find ladies constantly choosing to make their mental mediocrity more conspicuous by clothing it in a masquerade of ancient names; by putting their feeble sentimentality into the mouths of Roman vestals or Egyptian princesses, and attributing their rhetorical arguments to Jewish high priests and Greek philosophers. A recent example of this heavy imbecility is *Adonijah: A Tale of the Jewish Dispersion,** which forms part of a series, 'uniting', we are told, 'taste, humour and sound principles.' *Adonijah,* we presume, exemplifies the tale of 'sound principles'; the taste and humour are to be found in other members of the series. We are told on the cover that the incidents of this tale are 'fraught with unusual interest', and the preface winds up thus: 'To those who feel interested in the dispersed of

Israel and Judea, these pages may afford, perhaps, information on an important subject, as well as amusement.' Since the 'important subject' on which this book is to afford information is not specified, it may possibly lie in some esoteric meaning to which we have no key; but if it has relation to the dispersed of Israel and Judea at any period of their history, we believe a tolerably well-informed schoolgirl already knows much more of it than she will find in this *Tale of the Jewish Dispersion*. *Adonijah* is simply the feeblest kind of love story, supposed to be instructive, we presume, because the hero is a Jewish captive and the heroine a Roman vestal; because they and their friends are converted to Christianity after the shortest and easiest method approved by the 'Society for Promoting the Conversion of the Jews'; and because, instead of being written in plain language, it is adorned with that peculiar style of grandiloquence which is held by some lady novelists to give an antique colouring, and which we recognise at once in such phrases as these: 'the splendid regnal talent, undoubtedly, possessed by the Emperor Nero'; 'the expiring scion of a lofty stem'; 'the virtuous partner of his couch'; 'ah, by Vesta!'; and 'I tell thee, Roman'. Among the quotations which serve at once for instruction and ornament on the cover of this volume, there is one from Miss Sinclair,* which informs us that 'Works of imagination are avowedly read by men of science, wisdom and piety' − from which we suppose the reader is to gather the cheering inference that Dr Daubeny, Mr Mill or Mr Maurice* may openly indulge himself with the perusal of *Adonijah* without being obliged to secrete it among the sofa cushions, or read it by snatches under the dinner table.

'Be not a baker if your head be made of butter,' says a homely proverb, which, being interpreted, may mean, 'Let no woman rush into print who is not prepared for the consequences.' We are aware that our remarks are in a very different tone from that of the reviewers who, with perennial recurrence of precisely similar emotions, only paralleled, we imagine, in the experience of monthly nurses, tell one lady novelist after another that they 'hail' her productions 'with delight'. We are aware that the ladies at whom our criticism is pointed are accustomed to be told, in the choicest phraseology of puffery, that their pictures of life are brilliant, their characters well drawn, their style fascinating and their sentiments lofty. But if they are inclined to resent our plainness of speech, we ask them to reflect for a moment on the chary praise, and often captious blame, which their panegyrists give to writers whose works are on the way to become classics. No sooner does a woman show that she has genius or effective talent than she receives the tribute of being moderately praised and severely criticised. By a peculiar thermometric adjustment, when a woman's talent is at zero, journalistic approbation is at the boiling pitch; when she attains mediocrity, it is already at no more than summer heat; and if ever she reaches excellence, critical enthusiasm drops to the freezing point. Harriet Martineau, Currer Bell and Mrs Gaskell* have been treated as cavalierly as if they had been men. And every critic who forms a high estimate of the share women may ultimately take in literature will on principle abstain from any exceptional indulgence towards the productions of literary women. For it must be plain to everyone who looks impartially and extensively into feminine literature that its greatest deficiencies are due hardly more to the want of intellectual power than to the want of those moral qualities that contribute to literary excellence – patient diligence, a sense of the responsibility involved in publication and an appreciation of the sacredness of the writer's art. In the majority of women's books you see that kind of facility which springs from the absence of any high standard; that fertility in imbecile combination or feeble imitation which a little self-criticism would check and reduce to barrenness; just as with a total want of musical ear people will sing out of tune, while a degree more melodic sensibility would suffice to render them silent. The foolish vanity of wishing to appear in print, instead of being counterbalanced by any consciousness of the intellectual or moral derogation implied in futile authorship, seems to be encouraged by the extremely false impression that to write *at all* is a proof of superiority in a woman. On this ground we believe that the average intellect of women is unfairly represented by the mass of feminine literature, and that while the few women who write well are very far above the ordinary intellectual level of their sex, the many women who write ill are very far below it. So that, after all, the severer critics are fulfilling a chivalrous duty in depriving the mere fact of feminine authorship of any false prestige which may give it a delusive attraction, and in recommending women of mediocre faculties – as at least a negative service they can render their sex – to abstain from writing.

The standing apology for women who become writers without any special qualification is that society shuts them out from other spheres of occupation. Society is a very culpable entity, and has to answer for the manufacture of many unwholesome commodities, from bad pickles to bad poetry. But society, like 'matter', and Her Majesty's Government, and other lofty abstractions, has its share of excessive blame as well as excessive praise. Where there is one woman who writes from necessity, we believe there are three women who write from vanity; and besides, there is something so antiseptic in the mere healthy fact of working for one's bread that the most trashy and rotten kind of feminine literature is not likely to have been produced under such circumstances. 'In all labour there is profit';* but ladies' silly novels, we imagine, are less the result of labour than of busy idleness.

Happily, we are not dependent on argument to prove that Fiction is a department of literature in which women can, after their kind, fully equal men. A cluster of great names, both living and dead, rush to our memories in evidence that women can produce novels not only fine, but among the very finest – novels, too, that have a precious speciality, lying quite apart from masculine aptitudes and experience. No educational restrictions can shut women out from the materials of fiction, and there is no species of art which is so free from rigid requirements. Like crystalline masses, it may take any form and yet be beautiful; we have only to pour in the right elements – genuine observation, humour and passion. But it is precisely this absence of rigid requirement which constitutes the fatal seduction of novel-writing to incompetent women. Ladies are not wont to be very grossly deceived as to their power of playing on the piano; here certain positive difficulties of execution have to be conquered, and incompetence inevitably breaks down. Every art which had its absolute *technique* is, to a certain

extent, guarded from the intrusions of mere left-handed imbecility. But in novel-writing there are no barriers for incapacity to stumble against, no external criteria to prevent a writer from mistaking foolish facility for mastery. And so we have again and again the old story of La Fontaine's ass,[*] who pats his nose to the flute, and, finding that he elicits some sound, exclaims, '*Moi aussi, je joue de la flute*'[*] – a fable which we commend, at parting, to the consideration of any feminine reader who is in danger of adding to the number of 'silly novels by lady novelists'.

WOMAN IN FRANCE

*Madame de Sablé**

IN 1847, A CERTAIN COUNT LEOPOLD FERRI died at Padua, leaving a library entirely composed of works written by women, in various languages, and this library amounted to nearly 32,000 volumes. We will not hazard any conjecture as to the proportion of these volumes which a severe judge, like the priest in Don Quixote, would deliver to the flames,* but for our own part, most of these we should care to rescue would be the works of French women. With a few remarkable exceptions, our own feminine literature is made up of books which could have been better written by men – books which have the same relation to literature is general, as academic prize poems have to poetry: when not a feeble imitation, they are usually an absurd exaggeration of the masculine style, like the swaggering gait of a bad actress in male attire. Few English women have written so much like a woman as Richardson's Lady G.* Now we think it an immense mistake to maintain that there is no sex in literature. Science has no sex: the mere knowing and reasoning faculties, if they act correctly, must go through the same process, and arrive at the same result. But in art and literature, which imply the action of the entire being, in which every fibre of the nature is engaged, in which every peculiar modification of the individual makes itself felt, woman has something specific to contribute. Under every imaginable social condition, she will necessarily have a class of sensations and emotions – the maternal ones – which must remain unknown to man; and the fact of her comparative physical weakness, which, however it may have been exaggerated by a vicious civilisation, can never be cancelled, introduces a distinctively feminine condition into the wondrous chemistry of the affections and sentiments, which inevitably gives rise to distinctive forms and combinations. A certain amount of psychological difference between man and woman necessarily arises out of the difference of sex, and instead of being destined to vanish before a complete development of woman's intellectual and moral nature, will be a permanent source of variety and beauty as long as the tender light and dewy freshness of morning affect us differently from the strength and brilliancy of the midday sun. And those delightful women of France, who, from the beginning of the seventeenth to the close of the eighteenth century, formed some of the brightest threads in the web of political and literary history, wrote under circumstances which left the feminine character of their minds uncramped by timidity, and unstrained by mistaken effort. They were not trying to make a career for themselves; they thought little – in many cases not at all – of the public; they wrote letters to their lovers and friends, memoirs of their everyday lives, romances in which they gave portraits of their familiar acquaintances, and described the tragedy or comedy which was going on before their eyes. Always refined and graceful, often witty, sometimes judicious, they wrote what they saw, thought and felt in their habitual language, without proposing any model to themselves, without any intention to prove that women could write as well as men, without affecting manly views or suppressing womanly ones. One may say, at least with regard to the women of the seventeenth century, that their writings were but a charming accident of their more charming lives, like the petals which the wind shakes from the rose in its bloom. And it is but a twin fact with this that in France alone woman has had a vital influence on the development of literature; in France alone the mind of woman has passed like an electric current through the language, making crisp and definite what is elsewhere heavy and blurred; in France alone, if the writings of women were swept away, a serious gap would be made in the national history.

Patriotic gallantry may perhaps contend that English women could, if they had liked, have written as well as their neighbours; but we will leave the consideration of that question to the reviewers of the literature that might have been. In the literature that actually is, we must turn to France for the highest examples of womanly achievement in almost every department. We confess ourselves unacquainted with the productions of those awful women of Italy who held professorial chairs, and were great in civil and canon law; we have made no researches into the catacombs of female literature, but we think we may safely conclude that they would yield no rivals to that which is still unburied; and here, we suppose, the question of pre-eminence can only lie between England and France. And to this day, Madame de Sévigné* remains the single instance of a woman who is supreme in a class of literature which has engaged the ambition of men; Madame Dacier* still reigns the queen of bluestockings, though women have long studied Greek without shame;* Madame de Staël's* name still rises first to the lips when we are asked to mention a woman of great intellectual power; Madame Roland* is still the unrivalled type of the sagacious and sternly heroic, yet lovable woman; George Sand* is the unapproached artist who, to Jean-Jacques's* eloquence and deep sense of external nature, unites the clear delineation of character and the tragic depth of passion. These great names, which mark different epochs, soar like tall pines amidst a forest of less conspicuous, but not less fascinating, female writers; and beneath these, again, are spread, like a thicket of hawthorns, eglantines and honeysuckles, the women who are known rather by what they stimulated men to write, than by what they wrote themselves – the women whose tact, wit and personal radiance created the atmosphere of the *salon*, where literature, philosophy and science, emancipated from the trammels of pedantry and technicality, entered on a brighter stage of existence.

What were the causes of this earlier development and more abundant manifestation of womanly intellect in France? The primary one, perhaps, lies in the physiological characteristics of the Gallic race – the small brain and vivacious temperament which permit the fragile system of woman to sustain the superlative activity requisite for intellectual creativeness; while, on the other hand, the larger brain and slower temperament of the English and Germans are, in the womanly organisation, generally dreamy and passive. The type of humanity in the latter may be grander, but it requires a larger sum of conditions to produce a perfect specimen. Throughout the animal world, the higher the organisation, the more frequent is the departure from the normal form; we do not often see imperfectly developed or ill-made insects, but we rarely see a perfectly developed, well-made man. And thus the *physique* of a woman may suffice as the substratum for a superior Gallic mind, but is too thin a soil for a superior Teutonic one. Our theory is borne out by the fact that among our own countrywomen those who distinguish themselves by literary production more frequently approach the Gallic than the Teutonic type; they are intense and rapid rather than comprehensive. The woman of large capacity can seldom rise beyond the absorption of ideas; her physical conditions refuse to support the energy required for spontaneous activity; the voltaic-pile is not strong enough to produce crystallisations; phantasms of great ideas float through her mind, but she has not the spell which will arrest them and give them fixity. This, more than unfavourable external circumstances, is, we think, the reason why woman has not yet contributed any new form to art, any discovery in science, any deep-searching inquiry in philosophy. The necessary physiological conditions are not present in her. That under more favourable circumstances in the future these conditions may prove compatible with the feminine organisation, it would be rash to deny. For the present, we are only concerned with our theory so far as it presents a physiological basis for the intellectual effectiveness of French women.

A secondary cause was probably the laxity of opinion and practice with regard to the marriage tie. Heaven forbid that we should enter on a defence of French morals, most of all in relation to marriage! But it is undeniable that unions formed in the maturity of thought and feeling, and grounded only on inherent fitness and mutual attraction, tended to bring women into more intelligent sympathy with men, and to heighten and complicate their share in the political drama. The quiescence and security of the conjugal relation are doubtless favourable to the manifestation of the highest qualities by persons who have already attained a high standard of culture, but rarely foster a passion sufficient to rouse all the faculties to aid in winning or retaining its beloved object – to convert indolence into activity, indifference into ardent partisanship, dullness into perspicuity. Gallantry and intrigue are sorry enough things in themselves, but they certainly serve better to arouse the dormant faculties of woman than embroidery and domestic drudgery, especially when, as in the high society of France in the seventeenth century, they are refined by the influence of Spanish chivalry, and controlled by the spirit of Italian causticity. The dreamy and fantastic girl was awakened to reality by the experience of wifehood and maternity, and became capable of loving not a mere phantom of her own imagination, but a living man, struggling with the hatreds and rivalries of the political arena; she espoused his quarrels, she made herself, her fortune and her influence, the stepping stones of his ambition; and the languid beauty, who had formerly seemed ready to 'die of a rose',* was seen to become the heroine of an insurrection. The vivid interest in affairs which was thus excited in woman must obviously have tended to quicken her intellect, and give it a practical application; and the very sorrows – the heart pangs and regrets which are inseparable from a life of passion – deepened her nature by the questioning of self and destiny which they occasioned, and by the energy demanded to surmount them and live on. No wise person, we imagine, wishes to restore the social condition of France in the seventeenth century, or considers the ideal programme of woman's life to be a *marriage de convenance** at fifteen, a career of gallantry from twenty to eight-and-thirty, and penitence and piety for the rest of her days. Nevertheless, that social condition has its good results, as much as the madly superstitious Crusades had theirs.

But the most indisputable source of feminine culture and development in France was the influence of the *salons*, which, as all the world knows, were *réunions** of both sexes, where conversation ran along the whole gamut of subjects, from the frothiest *vers de société** to the philosophy of Descartes.* Richelieu* had set the fashion of uniting a taste for letters with the habits of polite society and the pursuits of ambition; and in the first quarter of the seventeenth century there were already several hotels in Paris, varying in social position from the closest proximity of the Court to the debatable ground of the aristocracy and the bourgeoisie, which served as a rendezvous for different circles of people, bent on entertaining themselves either by showing talent or admiring it. The most celebrated of these rendezvous was the Hôtel de Rambouillet, which was at the culmination of its glory in 1630,* and did not become quite extinct until 1648, when the troubles of the Fronde* commencing, its *habitués** were dispersed or absorbed by political interests. The presiding genius of this *salon*, the Marquise de Rambouillet, was the very model of the woman who can act as an amalgam to the most incongruous elements; beautiful, but not preoccupied by coquetry or passion; an enthusiastic admirer of talent, but with no pretensions to talent on her own part; exquisitely refined in language and manners, but warm and generous withal; not given to entertain her guests with her own compositions, or to paralyse them by her universal knowledge. She had once *meant* to learn Latin, but had been prevented by an illness; perhaps she was all the better acquainted with Italian and Spanish productions, which, in default of a national literature, were then the intellectual pabulum of all cultivated persons in France who are unable to read the classics. In her mild, agreeable presence was accomplished that blending of the high-toned chivalry of Spain with the caustic wit and refined irony of Italy, which issued in the creation of a new standard of taste – the combination of the utmost exaltation in sentiment with the utmost simplicity of language. Women are peculiarly fitted to further such a combination – first, from their greater tendency to mingle affection and imagination with passion, and thus subtilise it into sentiment; and next, from that dread of what overtaxes their intellectual energies, either by difficulty or monotony, which gives them an instinctive fondness for lightness of treatment and airiness of expression, thus making them cut short all prolixity and reject all heaviness. When these womanly characteristics were brought into conversational contact with the materials furnished by such minds as those of Richelieu, Corneille, the Great Condé, Balzac and Bossuet,* it is no wonder that the result was something piquant and charming. Those famous *habitués* of the Hôtel de Rambouillet did not, apparently, first lay themselves out to entertain the ladies with grimacing 'small talk' and then take each other by the sword knot to discuss matters of real interest in a corner; they rather sought to present their best ideas in the guise most acceptable to intelligent and accomplished women. And the conversation was not of literature only: war, politics, religion, the lightest details of daily news – everything was admissible, if only it were treated with refinement and intelligence. The Hôtel de Rambouillet was no mere literary *réunion*; it included *hommes d'affaires** and soldiers as well as authors, and in such a circle women would not become *bas bleus** or dreamy moralisers, ignorant of the world and of human nature, but intelligent observers of character and events. It is easy to understand, however, that with the herd of imitators who, in Paris and the provinces, aped the style of this famous *salon*, simplicity degenerated into affectation, and nobility of sentiment was replaced by an inflated effort to outstrip nature, so that the genre *précieux** drew down the satire, which reached its climax in the *Précieuses Ridicules* and *Les Femmes Savantes*, the former of which appeared in 1660, and the latter in 1673.* But Magdelon and Cathos are the lineal descendants of Mademoiselle Scudéry* and her satellites, quite as much as of the Hôtel de Rambouillet. The society which assembled every Saturday in her *salon* was exclusively literary, and although occasionally visited by a few persons of high birth, bourgeois in its tone and enamoured of madrigals, sonnets, stanzas and *bouts-rimés*.* The affectation that decks trivial things in fine language belongs essentially to a class which sees another above it, and is uneasy in the sense of its inferiority; and this affectation is precisely the opposite of the original genre *précieux*.

Another centre from which feminine influence radiated into the national literature was the Palais du Luxembourg, where Mademoiselle d'Orleans, in disgrace at court on account of her share in the Fronde,* held a little court of her own, and for want of anything else to employ her active spirit busied herself with literature. One fine morning it occurred to this princess to ask all the persons who frequented her court, among whom were Madame de Sévigné, Madame de la Fayette and La Rochefoucauld,* to write their own portraits, and she at once set the example. It was understood that defects and virtues were to be spoken of with like candour. The idea was carried out, those who were not clever or bold enough to write for themselves employing the pen of a friend.

Such (says M. Cousin)* was the pastime of Mademoiselle and her friends during the years 1657 and 1658: from this pastime proceeded a complete literature. In 1659 Ségrais revised these portraits, added a considerable number in prose and even in verse, and published the whole in a handsome quarto volume, admirably printed, and now become very rare, under the title *Divers Portraits*.* Only thirty copies were printed, not for sale, but to be given as presents by Mademoiselle. The work had a prodigious success. That which had made the fortune of Mademoiselle de Scudéry's romances – the pleasure of seeing one's portrait a little flattered, curiosity to see that of others, the passion which the middle class always have had and will have for knowing what goes on in the aristocratic world (at that time not very easy of access), the names of the illustrious persons who were here for the first time described physically and morally with the utmost detail, great ladies transformed all at once into writers, and unconsciously inventing a new manner of writing, of which no book gave the slightest idea, and which was the ordinary manner of speaking of the aristocracy; this undefinable mixture of the natural, the easy, and at the same time of the agreeable and supremely distinguished – all this charmed the court and the town, and very early in the year 1659 permission was asked of Mademoiselle to give a new edition of the privileged book for the use of the public in general.

The fashion thus set, portraits multiplied throughout France until, in 1688, La Bruyère adopted the form in his *Characters*,* and ennobled it by divesting it of personality. We shall presently see that a still greater work than La Bruyère's also owed its suggestion to a woman, whose *salon* was hardly a less fascinating resort than the Hôtel de Rambouillet itself.

In proportion as the literature of a country is enriched and culture becomes more generally diffused, personal influence is less effective in the formation of taste and in the furtherance of social advancement. It is no longer the coterie which acts on literature, but literature which acts on the coterie; the circle represented by the word *public* is ever widening, and ambition, poising itself in order to hit a more distant mark, neglects the successes of the *salon*. What was once lavished prodigally in conversation is reserved for the volume or the 'article', and the effort is not to betray originality rather than to communicate it. As the old coach roads have sunk into disuse through the creation of railways, so journalism tends more and more to divert information from the channel of conversation into the channel of the press; no one is satisfied with a more circumscribed audience than that very indeterminate abstraction 'the public', and men find a vent for their opinions not in talk, but in 'copy'. We read the *Athenaeum** askance at the tea-table, and take notes from the *Philosophical*

Journal* at a soirée; we invite our friends that we may thrust a book into their hands, and presuppose an exclusive desire in the 'ladies' to discuss their own matters, 'that we may crackle the *Times*' at our ease. In fact, the evident tendency of things to contract personal communication within the narrowest limits makes us tremble lest some further development of the electric telegraph should reduce us to a society of mutes, or to a sort of insects communicating by ingenious antenna of our own invention. Things were far from having reached this pass in the last century; but even then literature and society had outgrown the nursing of coteries, and although many *salons* of that period were worthy successors of the Hôtel de Rambouillet, they were simply a recreation, not an influence. Enviable evenings, no doubt, were passed in them; and if we could be carried back to any of them at will, we should hardly know whether to choose the Wednesday dinner at Madame Geoffrin's, with d'Alembert, Mademoiselle de l'Espinasse, Grimm and the rest, or the graver society which, thirty years later, gathered round Condorcet and his lovely young wife.* The *salon* retained its attractions, but its power was gone: the stream of life had become too broad and deep for such small rills to affect it.

A fair comparison between the French women of the seventeenth century and those of the eighteenth would, perhaps, have a balanced result, though it is common to be a partisan on this subject. The former have more exaltation, perhaps more nobility of sentiment, and less consciousness in their intellectual activity – less of the *femme auteur*,* which was Rousseau's horror in Madame d'Epinay;* but the latter have a richer fund of ideas – not more ingenuity, but the materials of an additional century for their ingenuity to work upon. The women of the seventeenth century, when love was on the wane, took to devotion, at first mildly and by halves, as English women take to caps, and finally without compromise; with the women of the eighteenth century, Bossuet and Massillon had given way to Voltaire and Rousseau;* and when youth and beauty failed, then they were thrown on their own moral strength.

M. Cousin is especially enamoured of the women of the seventeenth century, and relieves himself from his labours in philosophy by making researches into the original documents which throw light upon their lives. Last year he gave us some results of these researches in a volume on the youth of the Duchess de Longueville;* and he has just followed it up with a second volume, in which he further illustrates her career by tracing it in connection with that of her friend, Madame de Sablé. The materials to which he has had recourse for this purpose are chiefly two celebrated collections of manuscript: that of Conrart,* the first secretary to the French Academy, one of those universally curious people who seem made for the annoyance of contemporaries and the benefit of posterity; and that of Valant,* who was at once the physician, the secretary and general steward of Madame de Sablé, and who, with or without her permission, possessed himself of the letters addressed to her by her numerous correspondents during the latter part of her life, and of various papers having some personal or literary interest attached to them. From these stores M. Cousin has selected many documents previously unedited; and though he often leaves us something to desire in the arrangement of his materials, this volume of his on Madame de Sablé is very acceptable to us, for she interests us quite enough to carry us through more than three hundred pages of rather scattered narrative, and through an appendix of correspondence in small type. M. Cousin justly appreciates her character as '*un heureux mélange de raison, d'esprit, d'agrément et de bonté*';* and perhaps there are few better specimens of the woman who is extreme in nothing but sympathetic in all things; who affects us by no special quality, but by her entire being; whose nature has no *tons criards*,* but is like those textures which, from their harmonious blending of all colours, give repose to the eye, and do not weary us though we see them every day. Madame de Sablé is also a striking example of the one order of influence which woman has exercised over literature in France; and on this ground, as well as intrinsically, she is worth studying. If the reader agrees with us he will perhaps be inclined, as we are, to dwell a little on the chief points in her life and character.

Madeline de Souvré, daughter of the Marquis of Courtenvaux,* a nobleman distinguished enough to be chosen as governor of Louis XIII, was born in 1599, on the threshold of that seventeenth century, the brilliant genius of which is mildly reflected in her mind and history. Thus, when in 1635 her more celebrated friend, Mademoiselle de Bourbon, afterwards the Duchess de Longueville, made her appearance at the Hôtel de Rambouillet, Madame de Sablé had nearly crossed that tableland of maturity which precedes a woman's descent towards old age. She had been married in 1614, to Philippe Emanuel de Laval-Montmorency, Seigneur de Bois-Dauphin and Marquis de Sablé, of whom nothing further is known than that he died in 1640, leaving her the richer by four children, but with a fortune considerably embarrassed. With beauty and high rank added to the mental attractions of which we have abundant evidence, we may well believe that Madame de Sablé's youth was brilliant. For her beauty, we have the testimony of sober Madame de Motteville,* who also speaks of her as having '*beaucoup de lumière et de sincérité*';* and in the following passage very graphically indicates one phase of Madame de Sablé's character:

> The Marquise de Sablé was one of those whose beauty made the most noise when the Queen came into France. But if she was amiable, she was still more desirous of appearing so; this lady's self-love rendered her too sensitive to the regard which men exhibited towards her. There yet existed in France some remains of the politeness which Catherine de Medici* had introduced from Italy, and the new dramas, with all the other works in prose and verse, which came from Madrid, were thought to have such great delicacy, that she (Madame de Sablé) had conceived a high idea of the gallantry which the Spaniards had learned from the Moors.
>
> She was persuaded that men can, without crime, have tender sentiments for women – that the desire of pleasing them led men to the greatest and finest actions – roused their intelligence, and inspired them with liberality and all sorts of virtues; but, on the other hand, women, who were the ornament of the world, and made to be served and adored, ought not to admit anything from them but their respectful attentions. As this lady supported her views with much talent and great beauty, she had given them authority in her time, and the number and consideration of those who continued to associate with her have caused to subsist in our day what the Spaniards call *finezas*.*

Here is the grand element of the original *femme précieuse*,*
and it appears further, in a detail also reported by Madame
de Motteville, that Madame de Sablé had a passionate
admirer in the accomplished Duc de Montmorency,*
and apparently reciprocated his regard; but discovering
(at what period of their attachment is unknown) that he
was raising a lover's eyes towards the Queen, she broke
with him at once. 'I have heard her say,' tells Madame de
Motteville, 'that her pride was such with regard to the Duc
de Montmorency that at the first demonstrations which
he gave of his change, she refused to see him any more,
being unable to receive with satisfaction attentions which
she had to share with the greatest princess in the world.'
There is no evidence except the untrustworthy assertion
of Tallemant de Réaux* that Madame de Sablé had any
other *liaison* than this; and the probability of the negative
is increased by the ardour of her friendships. The strongest
of these was formed early in life with Mademoiselle Dona
d'Attichy, afterwards Comtesse de Maure;* it survived the
effervescence of youth, and the closest intimacy of middle
age, and was only terminated by the death of the latter in
1663. A little incident in this friendship is so characteristic
in the transcendentalism which was then carried into all the
affections that it is worth relating at length. Mademoiselle
d'Attichy, in her grief and indignation at Richelieu's treatment of her relative, quitted Paris, and was about to join
her friend at Sablé, when she suddenly discovered that
Madame de Sablé, in a letter to Madame de Rambouillet,
had said that her greatest happiness would be to pass her
life with Julie de Rambouillet, afterwards Madame de
Montausier.* To Anne d'Attichy this appears nothing less

than the crime of *lèse-amitié*.* No explanations will appease her: she refuses to accept the assurance that the offensive expression was used simply out of unreflecting conformity to the style of the Hôtel de Rambouillet – that it was mere '*galimatias*'.* She gives up her journey, and writes a letter, which is the only one Madame de Sablé chose to preserve, when, in her period of devotion, she sacrificed the records of her youth. Here it is:

> I have seen this letter in which you tell me there is so much *galimatias*, and I assure you that I have not found any at all. On the contrary, I find everything very plainly expressed, and, among others, one which is too explicit for my satisfaction – namely, what you have said to Madame de Rambouillet, that if you tried to imagine a perfectly happy life for yourself, it would be to pass it all alone with Mademoiselle de Rambouillet. You know whether anyone can be more persuaded than I am of her merit; but I confess to you that that has not prevented me from being surprised that you could entertain a thought which did so great an injury to our friendship. As to believing that you said this to one, and wrote it to the other, simply for the sake of paying them an agreeable compliment, I have too high an esteem for your courage to be able to imagine that complaisance would cause you thus to betray the sentiments of your heart, especially on a subject in which, as they were unfavourable to me, I think you would have the more reason for concealing them, the affection which I have for you being so well known to everyone, and especially to Mademoiselle de Rambouillet, so that I doubt whether she will not have been more sensible of the wrong

you have done me than of the advantage you have given her. The circumstance of this letter falling into my hands has forcibly reminded me of these lines of Bertaut:

Malheureuse est l'ignorance
Et plus malheureux le savoir.*

Having through this lost a confidence which alone rendered life supportable to me, it is impossible for me to take the journey so much thought of. For would there be any propriety in travelling sixty miles in this season, in order to burden you with a person so little suited to you that, after years of a passion without parallel, you cannot help thinking that the greatest pleasure of your life would be to pass it without her? I return, then, into my solitude, to examine the defects which cause me so much unhappiness, and unless I can correct them, I should have less joy than confusion in seeing you.

It speaks strongly for the charm of Madame de Sablé's nature that she was able to retain so susceptible a friend as Mademoiselle d'Attichy in spite of numerous other friendships, some of which, especially that with Madame de Longueville, were far from lukewarm – in spite, too, of a tendency in herself to distrust the affection of others towards her, and to wait for advances rather than to make them. We find many traces of this tendency in the affectionate remonstrances addressed to her by Madame de Longueville, now for shutting herself up from her friends, now for doubting that her letters are acceptable. Here is a little passage from one of these remonstrances which indicates a trait of

Madame de Sablé, and is in itself a bit of excellent sense, worthy the consideration of lovers and friends in general:

> I am very much afraid that if I leave to you the care of letting me know when I can see you, I shall be a long time without having that pleasure, and that nothing will incline you to procure it me, for I have always observed a certain lukewarmness in your friendship after our *explanations*, from which I have never seen you thoroughly recover; and that is why I dread explanations, for however good they may be in themselves, since they serve to reconcile people, it must always be admitted, to their shame, that they are at least the effect of a bad cause, and that if they remove it for a time they *sometimes leave a certain facility in getting angry again*, which, without diminishing friendship, renders its intercourse less agreeable. It seems to me that I find all this in your behaviour to me; so I am not wrong in sending to know if you wish to have me today.

It is clear that Madame de Sablé was far from having what Sainte-Beuve calls the one fault of Madame Necker* – absolute perfection. A certain exquisiteness in her physical and moral nature was, as we shall see, the source of more than one weakness, but the perception of these weaknesses, which is indicated in Madame de Longueville's letters, heightens our idea of the attractive qualities which notwithstanding drew from her, at the sober age of forty, such expressions as these: 'I assure you that you are the person in all the world whom it would be most agreeable to me to see, and there is no one whose intercourse is a ground of truer satisfaction to me. It is admirable that at all times, and amidst all changes, the taste for your society remains in me; and, *if one ought to thank God for the joys which do not tend to salvation*, I should thank him with all my heart for having preserved that to me at a time in which he has taken away from me all others.'

Since we have entered on the chapter of Madame de Sablé's weaknesses, this is the place to mention what was the subject of endless raillery from her friends – her elaborate precaution about her health, and her dread of infection, even from diseases the least communicable. Perhaps this anxiety was founded as much on aesthetic as on physical grounds, on disgust at the details of illness as much as on dread of suffering: with a cold in the head or a bilious complaint, the exquisite *précieuse* must have been considerably less conscious of being 'the ornament of the world' and 'made to be adored'. Even her friendship, strong as it was, was not strong enough to overcome her horror of contagion; for when Mademoiselle de Bourbon, recently become Madame de Longueville, was attacked by smallpox, Madame de Sablé for some time had not courage to visit her, or even to see Mademoiselle de Rambouillet, who was assiduous in her attendance on the patient. A little correspondence apropos of these circumstances so well exhibits the graceful badinage in which the great ladies of that day were adepts, that we are attempted to quote one short letter.

Mlle de Rambouillet to the Marquise de Sablé
Mlle de Chalais (*dame de compagnie* to the Marquise)* will please to read this letter to Mme la Marquise, *out of* a draught.

Madame,
I do not think it possible to begin my treaty with you too early, for I am convinced that between the first proposition

made to me that I should see you and the conclusion you will have so many reflections to make, so many physicians to consult and so many fears to surmount, that I shall have full leisure to air myself. The conditions which I offer to fulfil for this purpose are: not to visit you until I have been three days absent from the Hôtel de Condé (where Mme de Longueville was ill), to choose a frosty day, not to approach you within four paces, not to sit down on more than one seat. You may also have a great fire in your room, burn juniper in the four corners, surround yourself with imperial vinegar, with rue and wormwood. If you can feel yourself safe under these conditions, without my cutting off my hair, I swear to you to execute them religiously; and if you want examples to fortify you, I can tell you that the Queen consented to see M. Chaudebonne* when he had come directly from Mme de Bourbon's room, and that Mme d'Aiguillon, who has good taste in such matters, and is free from reproach on these points, has just sent me word that if I did not go to see her she would come to me.

Madame de Sablé betrays in her reply that she winces under this raillery, and thus provokes a rather severe though polite rejoinder, which, added to the fact that Madame de Longueville is convalescent, rouses her courage to the pitch of paying the formidable visit. Mademoiselle de Rambouillet, made aware through their mutual friend Voiture* that her sarcasm has cut rather too deep, winds up the matter by writing that very difficult production – a perfectly conciliatory yet dignified apology. Peculiarities like this always deepen with age, and accordingly, fifteen years later, we find Madame D'Orleans in her *Princesse de*

Paphlagonia* – a romance in which she describes her court, with the little quarrels and other affairs that agitated it – giving the following amusing picture, or rather caricature, of the extent to which Madame de Sablé carried her pathological mania, which seems to have been shared by her friend the Countess de Maure (Mademoiselle d'Attichy). In the romance, these two ladies appear under the names of Princesse Parthénie and the Reine de Mionie.

> There was not an hour in the day in which they did not confer together on the means of avoiding death, and on the art of rendering themselves immortal. Their conferences did not take place like those of other people; the fear of breathing an air which was too cold or too warm, the dread lest the wind should be too dry or too moist – in short, the imagination that the weather might not be as temperate as they thought necessary for the preservation of their health, caused them to write letters from one room to the other. It would be extremely fortunate if these notes could be found, and formed into a collection. I am convinced that they would contain rules for the regimen of life, precautions even as to the proper time for applying remedies, and also remedies which Hippocrates and Galen,* with all their science, never heard of. Such a collection would be very useful to the public, and would be highly profitable to the faculties of Paris and Montpellier. If these letters were discovered, great advantages of all kinds might be derived from them, for they were princesses who had nothing mortal about them but the *knowledge* that they were mortal. In their writings might be learned all politeness in style, and the most delicate manner of

speaking on all subjects. There is nothing with which they were not acquainted; they knew the affairs of all the States in the world, through the share they had in all the intrigues of its private members, either in matters of gallantry, as in other things, on which their advice was necessary; either to adjust embroilments and quarrels, or to excite them, for the sake of the advantages which their friends could derive from them; in a word, they were persons through whose hands the secrets of the whole world had to pass. The Princess Parthénie (Mme de Sablé) had a palate as delicate as her mind; nothing could equal the magnificence of the entertainments she gave; all the dishes were exquisite, and her cleanliness was beyond all that could be imagined. It was in their time that writing came into use; previously nothing was written but marriage contracts, and letters were never heard of; thus it is to them that we owe a practice so convenient in intercourse.

Still later, in 1669, when the most uncompromising of the Port-Royalists* seemed to tax Madame de Sablé with lukewarmness that she did not join them at Port-Royal-des-Champs, we find her writing to the stern M. de Sévigny: '*En vérité, je crois que je ne pourrois mieux faire que de tout quitter et de m'en aller là. Mais que deviendroient ces frayeurs de n'avoir pas de médicines à choisir, ni de chirurgien pour me saigner?*'*

Mademoiselle, as we have seen, hints at the love of delicate eating, which many of Madame de Sablé's friends numbered among her foibles, especially after her religious career had commenced. She had a genius in *friandise*,* and knew how to gratify the palate without offending the highest sense of refinement. Her sympathetic nature showed itself in this as in other things; she was always sending *bonnes bouches** to her friends, and trying to communicate to them her science and taste in the affairs of the table. Madame de Longueville, who had not the luxurious tendencies of her friend, writes: '*Je vous demande au nom de Dieu, que vous ne me prépariez aucun ragoût. Surtout ne me donnez point de festin. Au nom de Dieu, qu'il n'y ait rien que ce qu'on peut manger, car vous savez que c'est inutile pour moi; de plus j'en ai scrupule.*'* But other friends had more appreciation of her niceties. Voiture thanks her for her melons, and assures her that they are better than those of yesterday; Madame de Choisy hopes that her ridicule of Jansenism will not provoke Madame de Sablé to refuse her the receipt for salad; and La Rochefoucauld writes: 'You cannot do me a greater charity than to permit the bearer of this letter to enter into the mysteries of your marmalade and your genuine preserves, and I humbly entreat you to do everything you can in his favour. If I could hope for two dishes of those preserves, which I did not deserve to eat before, I should be indebted to you all my life.' For our own part, being as far as possible from fraternising with those spiritual people who convert a deficiency into a principle, and pique themselves on an obtuse palate as a point of superiority, we are not inclined to number Madame de Sablé's *friandise* among her defects. M. Cousin, too, is apologetic on this point. He says:

> It was only the excess of a delicacy which can be really understood, and a sort of fidelity to the character of *précieuse*. As the *précieuse* did nothing according to common usage, she could not dine like another. We have cited a passage from Mme de Motteville, where Mme de Sablé is represented in her first youth at the Hôtel de Rambouillet,

maintaining that woman is born to be an ornament to the world, and to receive the adoration of men. The woman worthy of the name ought always to appear above material wants, and retain, even in the most vulgar details of life, something distinguished and purified. Eating is a very necessary operation, but one which is not agreeable to the eye. Mme de Sablé insisted on its being conducted with a peculiar cleanliness. According to her it was not every woman who could with impunity be at table in the presence of a lover; the first distortion of the face, she said, would be enough to spoil all. Gross meals made for the body merely ought to be abandoned to *bourgeoises*, and the refined woman should appear to take a little nourishment merely to sustain her, and even to divert her, as one takes refreshments and ices. Wealth did not suffice for this: a particular talent was required. Mme de Sablé was a mistress in this art. She had transported the aristocratic spirit, and the genre *précieux*, good breeding and good taste, even into cookery. Her dinners, without any opulence, were celebrated and sought after.

It is quite in accordance with all this that Madame de Sablé should delight in fine scents, and we find that she did; for being threatened, in her Port-Royal days, when she was at an advanced age, with the loss of smell, and writing for sympathy and information to Mère Agnès, who had lost that sense early in life, she receives this admonition from the stern saint: 'You would gain by this loss, my very dear sister, if you made use of it as a satisfaction to God, for having had too much pleasure in delicious scents.' Scarron describes her as:

La non pareille Bois-Dauphine,
Entre dames perle très fine,*

and the superlative delicacy implied by this epithet seems to have belonged equally to her personal habits, her affections and her intellect.

Madame de Sablé's life, for anything we know, flowed on evenly enough until 1640, when the death of her husband threw upon her the care of an embarrassed fortune. She found a friend in Réné de Longueil, Seigneur de Maisons,* of whom we are content to know no more than that he helped Madame de Sablé to arrange her affairs, though only by means of alienating from her family the estate of Sablé, that his house was her refuge during the blockade of Paris in 1649,* and that she was not unmindful of her obligations to him, when, subsequently, her credit could be serviceable to him at court. In the midst of these pecuniary troubles came a more terrible trial – the loss of her favourite son, the brave and handsome Guy de Laval, who, after a brilliant career in the campaigns of Condé,* was killed at the siege of Dunkirk, in 1646, when scarcely four-and-twenty. The fine qualities of this young man had endeared him to the whole army, and especially to Condé, had won him the hand of the Chancellor Séguier's* daughter, and had thus opened to him the prospect of the highest honours. His loss seems to have been the most real sorrow of Madame de Sablé's life. Soon after followed the commotions of the Fronde, which put a stop to social intercourse, and threw the closest friends into opposite ranks. According to Lenet, who relies on the authority of Gourville,* Madame de Sablé was under strong obligations to the court, being in the receipt of a pension of 2000 crowns; at all events, she adhered throughout to the Queen and Mazarin, but being as far as possible from a fierce partisan, and given both by disposition and judgement to hear both sides of the question, she acted as a conciliator, and retained her friends of both parties. The Countess de Maure, whose husband was the most obstinate of *frondeurs*, remained throughout her most cherished friend, and she kept up a constant correspondence with the lovely and intrepid heroine of the Fronde, Madame de Longueville. Her activity was directed to the extinction of animosities, by bringing about marriages between the Montagues and Capulets of the Fronde – between the Prince de Condé, or his brother, and the niece of Mazarin, or between the three nieces of Mazarin and the sons of three noblemen who were distinguished leaders of the Fronde. Though her projects were not realised, her conciliatory position enabled her to preserve all her friendships intact, and when the political tempest was over, she could assemble around her in her residence, in the Place Royal, the same society as before. Madame de Sablé was now approaching her twelfth *lustrum*,* and though the charms of her mind and character made her more sought after than most younger women, it is not surprising that, sharing as she did in the religious ideas of her time, the concerns of 'salvation' seemed to become pressing. A religious retirement, which did not exclude the reception of literary friends or the care for personal comforts, made the most becoming frame for age and diminished fortune. Jansenism was then to ordinary Catholicism what Puseyism* is to ordinary Church of Englandism in these days – it was a *récherché** form of piety unshared by the vulgar; and one sees at once that it must have special attractions for the *précieuse*. Madame de Sablé, then, probably about 1655 or '56, determined to retire to Port-Royal, not because she was already devout, but because she hoped to become so; as, however, she wished to retain the pleasure of intercourse with friends who were still worldly, she built for herself a set of apartments at once distinct from the monastery and attached to it. Here, with a comfortable establishment, consisting of her secretary, Dr Valant, Mademoiselle de Chalais, formerly her *dame de compagnie* and now become her friend, an excellent cook, a few other servants and, for a considerable time, a carriage and coachman; with her best friends within a moderate distance, she could, as M. Cousin says, be out of the noise of the world without altogether forsaking it, preserve her dearest friendships, and have before her eyes edifying examples – '*vaquer enfin à son aise aux soins de son salut et à ceux de sa santé.*'*

We have hitherto looked only at one phase of Madame de Sablé's character and influence – that of the *précieuse*. But she was much more than this: she was the valuable, trusted friend of noblewomen and distinguished men; she was the animating spirit of a society, whence issued a new form of French literature; she was the woman of large capacity and large heart, whom Pascal sought to please, to whom Arnauld submitted the Discourse prefixed to his *Logic*, and to whom La Rochefoucauld writes: '*Vous savez que je ne crois que vous êtes sur de certains chapitres, et surtout sur les replis da cœur.*'* The papers preserved by her secretary, Valant, show that she maintained an extensive correspondence with persons of various rank and character; that her pen was untiring in the interest of others; that men made her the depositary of their thoughts, women of their sorrows; that her friends were as impatient, when she secluded herself, as if they had been rival lovers and she a youthful beauty. It is into her ear that Madame de Longueville pours her troubles and difficulties, and that Madame de la Fayette communicates her little alarms, lest young Count de St Paul should have detected her intimacy with La Rochefoucauld.* The few of Madame de Sablé's letters which survive show that she excelled in that epistolary style which was the specialty of the Hôtel de Rambouillet: one to Madame de Montausier, in favour of M. Périer, the brother-in-law of Pascal, is a happy mixture of good taste and good sense; but among them all we prefer quoting one to the Duchess de la Tremouille. It is light and pretty, and made out of almost nothing, like soap bubbles.

Je croix qu'il n'y a que moi qui face si bien tout le contraire de ce que je veux faire, car il est vrai qu'il n'y a personne que j'honore plus que vous, et j'ai si bien fait qu'il est quasi impossible que vous le puissiez croire. Ce n'estoit pas assez pour vous persuader que je suis indigne de vos bonnes grâces et de votre souvenir que d'avoir manqué fort longtemps à vous écrire; il falloit encore retarder quinze jours à me donner l'honneur de répondre à votre lettre. En vérité, Madame, cela me fait parôitre si coupable, que vers tout autre que vous j'aimeroix mieux l'être en effet que d'entreprendre une chose si difficile qu' est celle de me justifier. Mais je me sens si innocente dans mon âme, et j'ai tant d'estime, de respect et d'affection pour vous, qu'il me semble que vous devez le connôitre à cent lieues de distance d'ici, encore que je ne vous dise pas un mot. C'est ce que me donne le courage de vous écrire à cette heure, mais non pas ce qui m'en a empêché si longtemps. J'ai commencé, a faillir par force, ayant eu beaucoup de maux, et depuis je l'ai faite par honte, et je vous avoue que si je n'avois à cette heure la confiance que vous m'avez donnée en me rassurant, et celle que je tire de mes propres sentimens pour vous, je n'oserois jamais entreprendre de vous faire souvenir de moi; mais je m'assure que vous oublierez tout, sur la protestation que je vous fais de ne me laisser plus endurcir en mes fautes et de demeurer inviolablement, Madame, votre, etc.*

Was not the woman who could unite the ease and grace indicated by this letter, with an intellect that men thought worth consulting on matters of reasoning and philosophy, with warm affections, untiring activity for others, no ambition as an authoress, and an insight into *confitures* and *ragoûts*, a rare combination? No wonder that her *salon* at Port-Royal was the favourite resort of such women as Madame de la Fayette, Madame de Montausier, Madame de Longueville and Madame de Hautefort; and of such men as Pascal, La Rochefoucauld, Nicole and Domat.* The collections of Valant contain papers which show what were the habitual subjects of conversation in this *salon*. Theology, of course, was a chief topic; but physics and metaphysics had their turn, and still more frequently morals, taken in their widest sense. There were *Conferences on Calvinism*, of which an abstract is preserved. When Rohault invented his glass tubes* to serve for the barometrical experiments in which Pascal had roused a strong interest, the Marquis de Sourdis entertained the society with a paper entitled *Why Water Mounts in a Glass Tube*. Cartesianism was an exciting topic here, as well as everywhere else in France; it had its partisans and opponents, and papers were read, containing *Thoughts on the Opinions of M. Descartes*. These lofty matters were varied by discussions on love and friendship, on the drama, and on most of the things in heaven and earth which the philosophy of that day dreamed of. Morals – generalisations on human affections, sentiments and conduct – seem to have been the favourite theme; and the aim was to reduce these generalisations to their briefest form of expression, to give them the epigrammatic turn which made them portable in the memory. This was the specialty of Madame de Sablé's circle, and was, probably, due to her own tendency. As the Hôtel de Rambouillet was the nursery of graceful letter-writing, and the Luxembourg of 'portraits' and 'characters', so Madame de Sablé's *salon* fostered that taste for the sententious style, to which we owe, probably, some of the best *Pensées* of Pascal, and certainly the *Maxims* of La Rochefoucauld.* Madame de Sablé herself wrote maxims, which were circulated among her friends; and, after her death, were published by the Abbé d'Ailly. They have the excellent sense and nobility of feeling which we should expect in everything of hers; but they have no stamp of genius or individual character: they are, to the *Maxims* of La Rochefoucauld, what the vase moulded in dull, heavy clay is to the vase which the action of fire has made light, brittle and transparent. She also wrote a treatise on Education, which is much praised by La Rochefoucauld and M. d'Andilly;* but which seems no longer to be found: probably it was not much more elaborate than her so-called *Treatise on Friendship*, which is but a short string of maxims. Madame de Sablé's forte was evidently not to write herself, but to stimulate others to write; to show that sympathy and appreciation which are as genial and encouraging as the morning sunbeams. She seconded a man's wit with understanding – one of the best offices which womanly intellect has rendered to the advancement of culture; and the absence of originality made her all the more receptive towards the originality of others.

The manuscripts of Pascal show that many of the *Pensées*, which are commonly supposed to be raw materials for a great work on religion, were remodelled again and again, in order to bring them to the highest degree of terseness and finish, which would hardly have been the case if they had only been part of a quarry for a greater production. Thoughts, which are merely collected as materials, as stones out of which a building is to be erected, are not cut into facets, and polished like amethysts or emeralds. Since Pascal was from the first in the habit of visiting Madame de Sablé at Port-Royal, with his sister, Madame Périer (who was one of Madame de Sablé's dearest friends), we may well suppose that he would throw some of his jewels among the large and small coin of maxims, which were a sort of subscription money there. Many of them have an epigrammatical piquancy, which was just the thing to charm a circle of vivacious and intelligent women: they seem to come from a La Rochefoucauld who has been dipped over again in philosophy and wit, and received a new layer. But whether or not Madame de Sablé's influence served to enrich the *Pensées* of Pascal, it is clear that but for her influence the *Maxims* of La Rochefoucauld would never have existed. Just as in some circles the effort is, who shall make the best puns (*horibile dictu!*),* or the best charades, in the *salon* of Port-Royal the amusement was to fabricate maxims. La Rochefoucauld said, '*L'envie de faire des maximes se gagne comme la rhume.*'* So far from claiming for himself the initiation of this form of writing, he accuses Jacques Esprit,* another *habitué* of Madame de Sablé's *salon*, of having excited in him the taste for maxims, in order to trouble his repose. The said Esprit was an academician, and had been a frequenter of the Hôtel de Rambouillet. He had already published *Maxims in Verse*, and he subsequently produced a book called *La Faussete des vertus humaines*,* which seems to consist of Rochefoucauldism become flat with an infusion of sour Calvinism. Nevertheless, La Rochefoucauld seems to have prized him, to have appealed to his judgement, and to have concocted maxims with him, which he afterwards begs him to submit to Madame Sablé. He sends a little batch of maxims to her himself, and asks for an equivalent in the shape of good eatables: '*Voilà tout ce que j'ai de maximes; mais comme je ne donne rien pour rien, je vous demande un potage aux carottes, un ragoût de mouton,*'* etc. The taste and the talent enhanced each other until, at last, La Rochefoucauld began to be conscious of his pre-eminence in the circle of maxim-mongers, and thought of a wider audience. Thus grew up the famous *Maxims*, about which little need be said. Everyone at once is now convinced, or professes to be convinced, that as to form they are perfect, and that as to matter, they are at once undeniably true and miserably false; true as applied to that condition of human nature in which the selfish instincts are still dominant, false if taken as a representation of all the elements and possibilities of human nature. We think La Rochefoucauld himself wavered as to their universality, and that this wavering is indicated in the qualified form of some of the maxims; it occasionally struck him that the shadow of virtue must have a substance, but he had never grasped that substance – it had never been present to his consciousness.

It is curious to see La Rochefoucauld's nervous anxiety about presenting himself before the public as an author; far from rushing into print, he stole into it, and felt his way by asking private opinions. Through Madame de Sablé he sent manuscript copies to various persons of taste and talent, both men and women, and many of the written opinions which he received in reply are still in existence. The women generally find the maxims distasteful, but the men write approvingly. These men, however, are for the most part ecclesiastics, who decry human nature that they may exalt divine grace. The coincidence between Augustinianism or Calvinism, with its doctrine of human corruption, and the hard cynicism of the maxims, presents itself in quite a piquant form in some of the laudatory opinions on La Rochefoucauld. One writer says: '*On ne pourroit faire une instruction plus propre à un catechumène pour convertir à Dieu son esprit et sa volonté... Quand il n'y auroit que cet escrit au monde et l'Evangile je voudrois etre chretien. L'un m'apprendroit à connoistre mes misères, et l'autre à implorer mon libérateur.*'* Madame de Maintenon* sends word to La Rochefoucauld, after the publication of his work, that the Book of Job and the *Maxims* are her only reading.

That Madame de Sablé herself had a tolerably just idea of La Rochefoucauld's character, as well as of his maxims, may be gathered not only from the fact that her own maxims are as full of the confidence in human goodness which La Rochefoucauld wants as they are empty of the style which he possesses, but also from a letter in which she replies to the criticisms of Madame de Schomberg.* 'The author,' she says, 'derived the maxim on indolence from his own disposition, for never was there so great an indolence as his, and I think that his heart, inert as it is, owes this defect as much to his idleness as his will. It has never permitted him to do the least action for others; and I think that, amid all his great desires and great hopes, he is sometimes indolent even on his own behalf.' Still, she must have felt a hearty interest in the *Maxims*, as in some degree her foster-child, and she must also have had considerable affection for the author, who was lovable enough to those who observed the rule of Helvetius,* and expected nothing from him. She not only assisted him, as we have seen, in getting criticisms, and carrying out the improvements suggested by them, but when the book was actually published she prepared a notice of it for the only journal then existing – the *Journal des savants*.* This notice was originally a brief statement of the nature of the work, and the opinions which had been formed for and against it, with a moderate eulogy, in conclusion, on its good sense, wit and insight into human nature. But when she submitted it to La Rochefoucauld he objected to the paragraph which stated the adverse opinion, and requested her to alter it. She, however, was either unable or unwilling to modify her notice, and returned it with the following note:

Je vous envoie ce que j'ai pu tirer de ma teste pour mettre dans le Journal des savants. *J'y ai mis cet endroit qui vous est le plus sensible, afin que cela vous fasse surmonter la mauvaise honte qui vous fit mettre la préface sans y rien retrancher, et je n'ai pas craint dele mettre, parce que je suis assurée que vous ne le ferez pas imprimer, quand même le reste vous plairoit. Je vous assure aussi que je vous serai pins obligée, si vous en usez comme d'une chose qui servit à vous pour le corriger on pour le jeter au feu. Nous autres grands auteurs, nous sommes trop riches pour craindre de rien perdre de nos productions. Mandez-moi ce qu'il vous semble de ce dictum.**

La Rochefoucauld availed himself of this permission, and 'edited' the notice, touching up the style and leaving out the blame. In this revised form it appeared in the *Journal des savants*. In some points, we see, the youth of journalism was not without promise of its future.

While Madame de Sablé was thus playing the literary confidante to La Rochefoucauld, and was the soul of a society whose chief interest was the *belles-lettres*, she was equally active in graver matters. She was in constant intercourse or correspondence with the devout women of Port-Royal, and of the neighbouring convent of the Carmelites, many of whom had once been the ornaments of the court; and there is a proof that she was conscious of being highly valued by them in the fact that when the Princess Marie-Madeline of the Carmelites was dangerously ill, not being able or not daring to visit her, she sent her youthful portrait to be hung up in the sickroom, and received from the same Mère Agnès, whose grave admonition we have quoted above, a charming note, describing the pleasure which the picture had given in the infirmary of Notre Bonne Mère. She was interesting herself deeply in the translation of the New Testament, which was the work of Sacy, Arnauld, Nicole, Le Maître, and the Duc de Luynes* conjointly, Sacy having the principal share. We have mentioned that Arnauld asked her opinion on the Discourse prefixed to his *Logic*, and we may conclude from this that he had found her judgement valuable in many other cases. Moreover, the persecution of the Port-Royalists had commenced, and she was uniting with Madame de Longueville in aiding and protecting her pious friends. Moderate in her Jansenism, as in everything else, she held that the famous formulary denouncing the Augustinian doctrine, and declaring it to have been originated by Jansenius, should be signed without reserve, and, as usual, she had faith in conciliatory measures; but her moderation was no excuse for inaction. She was at one time herself threatened with the necessity of abandoning her residence at Port-Royal, and had thought of retiring to a religious house at Auteuil, a village near Paris. She did, in fact, pass some summers there, and she sometimes took refuge with her brother, the Commandeur de Souvré, with Madame de Montausier or Madame de Longueville. The last was much bolder in her partisanship than her friend, and her superior wealth and position enabled her to give the Port-Royalists more efficient aid. Arnauld and Nicole resided five years in her house; it was under her protection that the translation of the New Testament was carried on and completed, and it was chiefly through her efforts that, in 1669, the persecution was brought to an end. Madame de Sablé co-operated with all her talent and interest in the same direction; but here, as elsewhere, her influence was chiefly valuable in what she stimulated others to do, rather than in what she did herself. It was by her that Madame de Longueville was first won to the cause of Port-Royal; and we find this ardent brave woman constantly seeking the advice and sympathy of her more timid and self-indulgent, but sincere and judicious friend.

In 1669, when Madame de Sablé had at length rest from these anxieties, she was at the good old age of seventy, but she lived nine years longer – years, we may suppose, chiefly dedicated to her spiritual concerns. This gradual, calm decay allayed the fear of death, which had tormented her more vigorous days; and she died with tranquillity and trust. It is a beautiful trait of these last moments that she desired not to be buried with her family, or even at Port-Royal, among her saintly and noble companions – but in the cemetery of her parish, like one of the people, without pomp or ceremony.

It is worthwhile to notice that with Madame de Sablé, as with some other remarkable French women, the part of her life which is richest in interest and results is that which is looked forward to by most of her sex with melancholy as the period of decline. When between fifty and sixty, she had philosophers, wits, beauties and saints clustering around her; and one naturally cares to know what was the elixir which gave her this enduring and general attraction. We think it was, in a great degree, that well-balanced development of mental powers which gave her a comprehension of varied intellectual processes and a tolerance for varied forms of character, which is still rarer in women than in men. Here was one point of distinction between her and Madame de Longueville; and an amusing passage, which Sainte-Beuve has disinterred from the writings of the Abbé St Pierre, so well serves to indicate, by contrast, what we regard as the great charm of Madame de Sablé's mind, that we shall not be wandering from our subject in quoting it.

> I one day asked M. Nicole what was the character of Mme de Longueville's intellect; he told me it was very subtle and delicate in the penetration of character; but very small, very feeble, and that her comprehension was extremely narrow in matters of science and reasoning, and on all speculations that did not concern matters of sentiment. For example, he added, I one day said to her that I could wager and demonstrate that there were in Paris at least two inhabitants who had the same number of hairs, although I could not point out who these two men were. She told me I could never be sure of it until I had counted the hairs of these two men. Here is my demonstration, I said: I take it for granted that the head which is most amply supplied with hairs has not more than 200,000, and the head which is least so has but one hair. Now, if you suppose that 200,000 heads have each a different number of hairs, it necessarily follows that they have each one of the numbers

of hairs which form the series from one to 200,000; for if it were supposed that there were two among these 200,000 who had the same number of hairs, I should have gained my wager. Supposing, then, that these 200,000 inhabitants have all a different number of hairs, if I add a single inhabitant who has hairs, and who has not more than 200,000, it necessarily follows that this number of hairs, whatever it may be, will be contained in the series from one to 200,000, and consequently will be equal to the number of hairs on one of the previous 200,000 inhabitants. Now as, instead of one inhabitant more than 200,000, there are nearly 800,000 inhabitants in Paris, you see clearly that there must be many heads which have an equal number of hairs, though I have not counted them. Still, Mme de Longueville could never comprehend that this equality of hairs could be demonstrated, and always maintained that the only way of proving it was to count them.

Surely, the most ardent admirer of feminine shallowness must have felt some irritation when he found himself arrested by this dead wall of stupidity, and have turned with relief to the larger intelligence of Madame de Sablé, who was not the less graceful, delicate and feminine because she could follow a train of reasoning, or interest herself in a question of science. In this combination consisted her pre-eminent charm: she was not a genius, not a heroine, but a woman whom men could more than love – whom they could make their friend, confidante and counsellor; the sharer not of their joys and sorrows only, but of their ideas and aims.

Such was Madame de Sablé, whose name is, perhaps, new to some of our readers, so far does it lie from the surface of literature and history. We have seen, too, that she was only one among a crowd – one in a firmament of feminine stars which, when once the biographical telescope is turned upon them, appear scarcely less remarkable and interesting. Now, if the reader recollects what was the position and average intellectual character of women in the high society of England during the reigns of James the First and the two Charleses* – the period through which Madame de Sablé's career extends – we think he will admit our position as to the early superiority of womanly development in France, and this fact, with its causes, has not merely an historical interest: it has an important bearing on the culture of women in the present day. Women become superior in France by being admitted to a common fund of ideas, to common objects of interest with men; and this must ever be the essential condition at once of true womanly culture and of true social well-being. We have no faith in feminine conversazioni, where ladies are eloquent on Apollo and Mars; though we sympathise with the yearning activity of faculties which, deprived of their proper material, waste themselves in weaving fabrics out of cobwebs. Let the whole field of reality be laid open to woman, as well as to man, and then that which is peculiar in her mental modification, instead of being, as it is now, a source of discord and repulsion between the sexes, will be found to be a necessary complement to the truth and beauty of life. Then we shall have that marriage of minds which alone can blend all the hues of thought and feeling in one lovely rainbow of promise for the harvest of human happiness.

THE GRAMMAR OF ORNAMENT*

THE INVENTOR OF MOVABLE TYPES, says the venerable Teufelsdröckh,* was disbanding hired armies, cashiering most kings and senates and creating a whole new democratic world. Has anyone yet said what great things are being done by the men who are trying to banish ugliness from our streets and our homes, and to make both the outside and inside of our dwellings worthy of a world where there are forests and flower-tressed meadows, and the plumage of birds; where the insects carry lessons of colour on their wings, and even the surface of a stagnant pool will show us the wonders of iridescence and the most delicate forms of leafage? They, too, are modifying opinions, for they are modifying men's moods and habits, which are the mothers of opinions, having quite as much to do with their formation as the responsible father, Reason. Think of certain hideous manufacturing towns where the piety is chiefly a belief in copious perdition, and the pleasure is chiefly gin. The dingy surface of wall pierced by the ugliest windows, the staring shopfronts, paper-hangings, carpets, brass and gilded mouldings and advertising placards, have an effect akin to that of malaria; it is easy to understand that with such surroundings there is more belief in cruelty than in beneficence, and that the best earthly bliss attainable is the dulling of the external senses. For it is a fatal mistake to suppose that ugliness which is taken for beauty will answer all the purposes of beauty; the subtle relation between all kinds of truth and fitness in our life forbids that bad taste should ever be harmless to our moral sensibility or our intellectual discernment; and − more than that − as it is probable that fine musical harmonies have a sanative influence over our bodily organisation, it is also probable that just colouring and lovely combinations of lines may be necessary to the complete well-being of our systems apart from any conscious delight in them. A savage may indulge in discordant chuckles and shrieks and gutturals, and think that they please the gods, but it does not follow that his frame would not be favourably wrought upon by the vibrations of a grand church organ. One sees a person capable of choosing the worst style of wallpaper become suddenly afflicted by its ugliness under an attack of illness. And if an evil state of blood and lymph usually goes along with an evil state of mind, who shall say that the ugliness of our streets, the falsity of our ornamentation, the vulgarity of our upholstery, have not something to do with those bad tempers which breed false conclusions?

On several grounds it is possible to make a more speedy and extensive application of artistic reform to our interior decoration than to our external architecture. One of these grounds is that most of our ugly buildings must stand; we cannot afford to pull them down. But every year we are decorating interiors afresh, and people of modest means may benefit by the introduction of beautiful designs into stucco ornaments, paper-hangings, draperies and carpets. Fine taste in the decoration of interiors is a benefit that spreads from the palace to the clerk's house with one parlour.

All honour, then, to the architect who has zealously vindicated the claim of internal ornamentation to be a part of the architect's function, and has laboured to rescue that form of art which is most closely connected with the sanctities and pleasures of our hearths from the hands of uncultured tradesmen. All the nation ought at present to know that this effort is peculiarly associated with the name of Mr Owen Jones; and those who are most disposed to dispute with the architect about his colouring must at least recognise the high artistic principle which has directed his attention to coloured ornamentation as a proper branch of architecture. One monument of his effort in this way is his *Grammar of Ornament*, of which a new and cheaper edition has just been issued. The one point in which it differs from the original and more expensive edition, viz., the reduction in the size of the pages (the amount of matter and number of plates are unaltered), is really an advantage; it is now a very manageable folio, and when the reader is in a lounging mood may be held easily on the knees. It is a magnificent book; and those who know no more of it than the title should be told that they will find in it a pictorial history of ornamental design, from its rudimentary condition as seen in the productions of savage tribes, through all the other great types of art – the Egyptian, Assyrian, ancient Persian, Greek, Roman, Byzantine, Arabian, Moresque, Mohammedan-Persian, Indian, Celtic, Medieval, Renaissance, Elizabethan and Italian. The letter-press consists, first, of an introductory statement of fundamental principles of ornamentation – principles, says the author, which will be found to have been obeyed more or less instinctively by all nations in proportion as their art has been a genuine product of the national genius; and, secondly, of brief historical essays, some of them contributed by other eminent artists, presenting a commentary on each characteristic series of illustrations, with the useful appendage of bibliographical lists.

The title, *Grammar of Ornament*, is so far appropriate that it indicates what Mr Owen Jones is most anxious to be understood concerning the object of his work – namely, that it is intended to illustrate historically the application of principles, and not to present a collection of models for mere copyists. The plates correspond to examples in syntax, not to be repeated parrot-like, but to be studied as embodiments of syntactical principles. There is a logic of form which cannot be departed from in ornamental design without a corresponding remoteness from perfection; unmeaning, irrelevant lines are as bad as irrelevant words or clauses, that tend no whither. And as a suggestion towards the origination of fresh ornamental design, the work concludes with some beautiful drawings of leaves and flowers from nature, that the student, tracing in them the simple laws of form which underlie an immense variety in beauty, may the better discern the method by which the same laws were applied in the finest decorative work of the past, and may have all the clearer prospect of the unexhausted possibilities of freshness which lie before him, if, refraining from mere imitation, he will seek only such likeness to existing forms of ornamental art as arises from following like principles of combination.

THE TOO-READY WRITER

ONE WHO TALKS TOO MUCH, hindering the rest of the company from taking their turn, and apparently seeing no reason why they should not rather desire to know his opinion or experience in relation to all subjects, or at least to renounce the discussion of any topic where he can make no figure, has never been praised for this industrious monopoly of work which others would willingly have shared in. However various and brilliant his talk may be, we suspect him of impoverishing us by excluding the contributions of other minds, which attract our curiosity the more because he has shut them up in silence. Besides, we get tired of a 'manner' in conversation as in painting, when one theme after another is treated with the same lines and touches. I begin with a liking for an estimable master, but by the time he has stretched his interpretation of the world unbrokenly along a palatial gallery, I have had what the cautious Scotch mind would call 'enough' of him. There is monotony and narrowness already to spare in my own identity; what comes to me from without should be larger and more impartial than the judgement of any single interpreter. On this ground even a modest person, without power or will to shine in the conversation, may easily find the predominating talker a nuisance, while those who are full of matter on special topics are continually detecting miserably thin places in the web of that information which he will not desist from imparting. Nobody that I know of ever proposed a testimonial to a man for thus volunteering the whole expense of the conversation.

Why is there a different standard of judgement with regard to a writer who plays much the same part in literature as the excessive talker plays in what is traditionally called conversation? The busy Adrastus, whose professional engagements might seem more than enough for the nervous energy of one man, and who yet finds time to print essays on the chief current subjects, from the tri-lingual inscriptions, or the Idea of the Infinite among the prehistoric Lapps, to the Colorado beetle and the grape disease in the south of France, is generally praised if not admired for the breadth of his mental range and his gigantic powers of work. Poor Theron, who has some original ideas on a subject to which he has given years of research and meditation, has been waiting anxiously from month to month to see whether his condensed exposition will find a place in the next advertised programme, but sees it, on the contrary, regularly excluded, and twice the space he asked for filled with the copious brew of Adrastus, whose name carries custom like a celebrated trademark. Why should the eager haste to tell what he thinks on the shortest notice, as if his opinion were a needed preliminary to discussion, get a man the reputation of being a conceited bore in conversation, when nobody blames the same tendency if it shows itself in print? The excessive talker can only be in one gathering at a time, and there is the comfort of thinking that everywhere else other fellow citizens who have something to say may get a chance of delivering themselves; but the exorbitant writer can occupy space and spread over it the more or less agreeable flavour of his mind in four 'mediums' at once, and on subjects taken from the four winds. Such restless and versatile occupants of literary space and time should have lived earlier when the world wanted summaries of all extant knowledge, and this knowledge being small, there was the more room for commentary and conjecture. They might have played the part of an Isidore of Seville or a Vincent of Beauvais* brilliantly, and the willingness to write everything themselves would have been strictly in place. In the present day, the busy retailer of other people's knowledge which he has spoiled in the handling, the restless guesser and commentator, the importunate hawker of undesirable superfluities, the everlasting word-compeller who rises early in the morning to praise what the world has already glorified, or makes himself haggard at night in writing out his dissent from what nobody ever believed, is not simply *'gratis anhelans, multa agendo nihil agens'** – he is an obstruction. Like an incompetent architect with too much interest at his back, he obtrudes his ill-considered work where place ought to have been left to better men.

Is it out of the question that we should entertain some scruple about mixing our own flavour, as of the too cheap and insistent nutmeg, with that of every great writer and every great subject? Especially when our flavour is all we have to give, the matter or knowledge having been already given by somebody else. What if we were only like the Spanish wineskins which impress the innocent stranger with the notion that the Spanish grape has naturally a taste of leather? One could wish that even the greatest minds should leave some themes unhandled – or at least leave us no more than a paragraph or two on them to show how well they did in not being more lengthy.

Such entertainment of scruple can hardly be expected from the young; but happily their readiness to mirror the universe anew for the rest of mankind is not encouraged by easy publicity. In the vivacious Pepin I have often seen the image of my early youth, when it seemed to me astonishing that the philosophers had left so many difficulties unsolved, and that so many great themes had raised no great poet to treat them. I had an elated sense that I should find my brain full of theoretic clues when I looked for them, and that wherever a poet had not done what I expected, it was for want of my insight. Not knowing what had been said about the play of *Romeo and Juliet*, I felt myself capable of writing something original on its blemishes and beauties. In relation to all subjects I had a joyous consciousness of that ability which is prior to knowledge, and of only needing to apply myself in order to master any task – to conciliate philosophers whose systems were at present but dimly known to me, to estimate foreign poets whom I had not yet read, to show up mistakes in an historical monograph that roused my interest in an epoch which I had been hitherto ignorant of, when I should once have had time to verify my views of probability by looking into an encyclopaedia. So Pepin; save only that he is industrious while I was idle. Like the astronomer in *Rasselas*,* I swayed the universe in my consciousness without making any difference outside me; whereas Pepin, while feeling himself powerful with the stars in their courses, really raises some dust here below. He is no longer in his spring tide, but having been always busy he has been obliged to use his first impressions as if they were deliberate opinions, and to range himself on the corresponding side in ignorance of much that he commits himself to; so that he retains some characteristics of a comparatively tender age, and among them a certain surprise that there have not been more persons equal to himself. Perhaps it is unfortunate for him that he early gained a hearing, or at least a place in print, and was thus encouraged in acquiring a fixed habit of writing, to the exclusion of any other breadwinning pursuit. He is already to be classed as a 'general writer', corresponding to the comprehensive wants of the 'general reader', and with this industry on his hands it is not enough for him to keep up the ingenuous self-reliance of youth: he finds himself under an obligation to be skilled in various methods of seeming to know; and having habitually expressed himself before he was convinced, his interest in all subjects is chiefly to ascertain that he has not made a mistake, and to feel his infallibility confirmed. That impulse to decide, that vague sense of being able to achieve the unattempted, that dream of aerial unlimited movement at will without feet or wings, which were once but the joyous mounting of young sap, are already taking shape as unalterable woody fibre: the impulse has hardened into 'style', and into a pattern of peremptory sentences; the sense of ability in the presence of other men's failures is turning into the official arrogance of one who habitually issues directions which he has never himself been called on to execute; the dreamy buoyancy of the stripling has taken on a fatal sort of reality in written pretensions which carry consequences. He is on the way to become like the loud-buzzing, bouncing Bombus, who combines conceited illusions enough to supply several patients in a lunatic asylum with the freedom to show himself at large in various forms of print. If one who takes himself for the telegraphic centre of all American wires is to be confined as unfit to transact affairs, what shall we say to the man who believes himself in possession of the unexpressed motives and designs dwelling in the breasts of all sovereigns and all politicians? And I grieve to think that poor Pepin, though less political, may by and by manifest a persuasion hardly more sane, for he is beginning to explain people's writing by what he does not know about them. Yet he was once at the comparatively innocent stage which I have confessed to be that of my own early astonishment at my powerful originality; and copying the just humility of the old Puritan, I may say, 'But for the grace of discouragement, this coxcombry might have been mine.'

Pepin made for himself a necessity of writing (and getting printed) before he had considered whether he had the knowledge or belief that would furnish eligible matter. At first, perhaps, the necessity galled him a little, but it is now as easily borne – nay, is as irrepressible a habit as the outpouring of inconsiderate talk. He is gradually being condemned to have no genuine impressions, no direct consciousness of enjoyment or the reverse from the quality of what is before him: his perceptions are continually arranging themselves in forms suitable to a printed judgement, and hence they will often turn out to be as much to the purpose if they are written without any direct contemplation of the object, and are guided by a few external conditions which serve to classify it for him. In this way he is irrevocably losing the faculty of accurate mental vision: having bound himself to express judgements which will satisfy some other demands than that of veracity, he has blunted his perceptions by continual preoccupation. We cannot command veracity at will: the power of seeing and reporting truly is a form of health that has to be delicately guarded, and as an ancient Rabbi has solemnly said, 'The penalty of untruth is untruth.'* But Pepin is only a mild example of the fact that incessant writing with a view to printing carries internal consequences which have often the nature of disease. And however unpractical it may be held to consider whether we have anything to print which it is good for the world to read, or which has not been better said before, it will perhaps be allowed to be worth considering what effect the printing may have on ourselves. Clearly there is a sort of writing which helps to keep the writer in a ridiculously contented ignorance; raising in him continually the sense of having delivered himself effectively, so that the acquirement of more thorough knowledge seems as superfluous as the purchase of costume for a past occasion. He has invested his vanity (perhaps his hope of income) in his own shallownesses and mistakes, and must desire their prosperity. Like the professional prophet, he learns to be glad of the harm that keeps up his credit, and to be sorry for the good that contradicts him. It is hard enough for any of us, amid the changing winds of fortune and the hurly-burly of events, to keep quite clear of a gladness which is another's calamity; but one may choose not to enter on a course which will turn such gladness into a fixed habit of mind, committing ourselves to be continually pleased that others should appear to be wrong in order that we may have the air of being right.

In some cases, perhaps, it might be urged that Pepin has remained the more self-contented because he has *not* written everything he believed himself capable of. He once asked me to read a sort of programme of the species of romance which he should think it worthwhile to write – a species which he contrasted in strong terms with the productions of illustrious but overrated authors in this branch. Pepin's romance was to present the splendours of the Roman Empire at the culmination of its grandeur, when decadence was spiritually but not visibly imminent: it was to show the workings of human passion in the most pregnant and exalted of human circumstances, the designs of statesmen, the interfusion of philosophies, the rural relaxation and converse of immortal poets, the majestic triumphs of warriors, the mingling of the quaint and sublime in religious ceremony, the gorgeous delirium of gladiatorial shows, and under all the secretly working leaven of Christianity. Such a romance would not call the attention of society to the dialect of stable boys, the low habits of rustics, the vulgarity of small schoolmasters, the manners of men in livery or to any other form of uneducated talk and sentiments: its characters would have virtues and vices alike on the grand scale, and would express themselves in an English representing the discourse of the most powerful minds in the best Latin, or possibly Greek, when there occurred a scene with a Greek philosopher on a visit to Rome or resident there as a teacher. In this way Pepin would do in fiction what had never been done before: something not at all like *Rienzi* or *Notre Dame de Paris*,* or any other attempt of that kind; but something at once more penetrating and more magnificent, more passionate and more philosophical, more panoramic yet more select: something that would present a conception of a gigantic period; in short something truly Roman and world-historical.

THE TOO-READY WRITER

When Pepin gave me this programme to read he was much younger than at present. Some slight success in another vein diverted him from the production of panoramic and select romance, and the experience of not having tried to carry out his programme has naturally made him more biting and sarcastic on the failures of those who have actually written romances without apparently having had a glimpse of a conception equal to his. Indeed, I am often comparing his rather touchingly inflated *naïveté* as of a small young person walking on tiptoe while he is talking of elevated things, at the time when he felt himself the author of that unwritten romance, with his present epigrammatic curtness and affectation of power kept strictly in reserve. His paragraphs now seem to have a bitter smile in them, from the consciousness of a mind too penetrating to accept any other man's ideas, and too equally competent in all directions to seclude his power in any one form of creation, but rather fitted to hang over them all as a lamp of guidance to the stumblers below. You perceive how proud he is of not being indebted to any writer: even with the dead he is on the creditor's side, for he is doing them the service of letting the world know what they meant better than those poor pre-Pepinians themselves had any means of doing, and he treats the mighty shades very cavalierly.

Is this fellow citizen of ours, considered simply in the light of a baptised Christian and tax-paying Englishman, really as madly conceited, as empty of reverential feeling, as unveracious and careless of justice, as full of catch-penny devices and stagey attitudinising as on examination his writing shows itself to be? By no means. He has arrived at his present pass in 'the literary calling' through the self-imposed obligation to give himself a manner which would convey the impression of superior knowledge and ability. He is much worthier and more admirable than his written productions, because the moral aspects exhibited in his writing are felt to be ridiculous or disgraceful in the personal relations of life. In blaming Pepin's writing we are accusing the public conscience, which is so lax and ill-informed on the momentous bearings of authorship that it sanctions the total absence of scruple in undertaking and prosecuting what should be the best warranted of vocations.

Hence I still accept friendly relations with Pepin, for he has much private amiability, and though he probably thinks of me as a man of slender talents, without rapidity of *coup d'oeil** and with no compensatory penetration, he meets me very cordially, and would not, I am sure, willingly pain me in conversation by crudely declaring his low estimate of my capacity. Yet I have often known him to insult my betters and contribute (perhaps unreflectingly) to encourage injurious conceptions of them – but that was done in the course of his professional writing, and the public conscience still leaves such writing nearly on the level of the merry-andrew's dress,* which permits an impudent deportment and extraordinary gambols to one who in his ordinary clothing shows himself the decent father of a family.

DISEASES OF SMALL AUTHORSHIP

PARTICULAR CALLINGS, it is known, encourage particular diseases. There is a painter's colic; the Sheffield grinder falls a victim to the inhalation of steel dust; clergymen so often have a certain kind of sore throat that this otherwise secular ailment gets named after them. And perhaps, if we were to inquire, we should find a similar relation between certain moral ailments and these various occupations, though here in the case of clergymen there would be specific differences: the poor curate, equally with the rector, is liable to clergyman's sore throat, but he would probably be found free from the chronic moral ailments encouraged by the possession of glebe and those higher chances of preferment which follow on having a good position already. On the other hand, the poor curate might have severe attacks of calculating expectancy concerning parishioners' turkeys, cheeses and fat geese, or of uneasy rivalry for the donations of clerical charities.

Authors are so miscellaneous a class that their personified diseases, physical and moral, might include the whole procession of human disorders, led by dyspepsia and ending in madness – the awful Dumb Show of a world-historic tragedy. Take a large enough area of human life and all comedy melts into tragedy, like the Fool's part by the side of Lear. The chief scenes get filled with erring heroes, guileful usurpers, persecuted discoverers, dying deliverers: everywhere the protagonist has a part pregnant with doom. The comedy sinks to an accessory, and if there are loud laughs they seem a convulsive transition from sobs; or if the comedy is touched with a gentle lovingness, the panoramic scene is one where

> Sadness is a kind of mirth
> So mingled as if mirth did make us sad
> And sadness merry. *

But I did not set out on the wide survey that would carry me into tragedy, and in fact had nothing more serious in my mind than certain small chronic ailments that come of small authorship. I was thinking principally of Vorticella, who flourished in my youth not only as a portly lady walking in silk attire, but also as the authoress of a book entitled *The Channel Islands, with Notes and an Appendix*. I would by no means make it a reproach to her that she wrote no more than one book; on the contrary, her stopping there seems to me a laudable example. What one would have wished, after experience, was that she had refrained from producing even that single volume, and thus from giving her self-importance a troublesome kind of double incorporation which became oppressive to her acquaintances, and set up in herself one of those slight chronic forms of disease to which I have just referred.

DISEASES OF SMALL AUTHORSHIP

She lived in the considerable provincial town of Pumpiter, which had its own newspaper press, with the usual divisions of political partisanship and the usual varieties of literary criticism – the florid and allusive, the *staccato* and peremptory, the clairvoyant and prophetic, the safe and pattern-phrased, or what one might call 'the many-a-long-day style'.

Vorticella being the wife of an important townsman had naturally the satisfaction of seeing *The Channel Islands* reviewed by all the organs of Pumpiter opinion, and their articles or paragraphs held as naturally the opening pages in the elegantly bound album prepared by her for the reception of 'critical opinions'. This ornamental volume lay on a special table in her drawing room, close to the still-more-gorgeously-bound work of which it was the significant effect, and every guest was allowed the privilege of reading what had been said of the authoress and her work in the *Pumpiter Gazette and Literary Watchman*, the *Pumpshire Post*, the *Church Clock*, the *Independent Monitor* and the lively but judicious publication known as the *Medley Pie*; to be followed up, if he chose, by the instructive perusal of the strikingly confirmatory judgements, sometimes concurrent in the very phrases, of journals from the most distant counties; as the *Latchgate Argus*, the *Penllwy Universe*, the *Cockaleekie Advertiser*, the *Goodwin Sands Opinion* and the *Land's End Times*.

I had friends in Pumpiter and occasionally paid a long visit there. When I called on Vorticella, who had a cousinship with my hosts, she had to excuse herself because a message claimed her attention for eight or ten minutes, and, handing me the album of critical opinions, said, with a certain emphasis which, considering my youth, was highly complimentary, that she would really like me to read what I should find there. This seemed a permissive politeness which I could not feel to be an oppression, and I ran my eyes over the dozen pages, each with a strip or islet of newspaper in the centre, with that freedom of mind (in my case meaning freedom to forget) which would be a perilous way of preparing for examination. This *ad libitum* perusal had its interest for me. The private truth being that I had not read *The Channel Islands*, I was amazed at the variety of matter which the volume must contain to have impressed these different judges with the writer's surpassing capacity to handle almost all branches of inquiry and all forms of presentation. In Jersey she had shown herself an historian, in Guernsey a poetess, in Alderney a political economist and in Sark a humorist: there were sketches of character scattered through the pages which might put our 'fictionists' to the blush; the style was eloquent and racy, studded with gems of felicitous remark; and the moral spirit throughout was so superior that, said one, 'the recording angel' (who is not supposed to take account of literature as such) 'would assuredly set down the work as a deed of religion.' The force of this eulogy on the part of several reviewers was much heightened by the incidental evidence of their fastidious and severe taste, which seemed to suffer considerably from the imperfections of our chief writers, even the dead and canonised: one afflicted them with the smell of oil, another lacked erudition and attempted (though vainly) to dazzle them with trivial conceits, one wanted to be more philosophical than nature had made him, another in attempting to be comic produced the melancholy effect of a half-starved merry-andrew; while one and all, from the author of the *Areopagitica** downwards, had faults of style which must have made an able hand in the *Latchgate Argus* shake the many-glanced head belonging thereto with a smile of compassionate disapproval. Not so the authoress of *The Channel Islands*: Vorticella and Shakespeare were allowed to be faultless. I gathered that no blemishes were observable in the work of this accomplished writer, and the repeated information that she was 'second to none' seemed after this superfluous. Her thick octavo – notes, appendix and all – was unflagging from beginning to end; and the *Land's End Times*, using a rather dangerous rhetorical figure, recommended you not to take up the volume unless you had leisure to finish it at a sitting. It had given one writer more pleasure than he had had for many a long day – a sentence which had a melancholy resonance, suggesting a life of studious languor such as all previous achievements of the human mind failed to stimulate into enjoyment. I think the collection of critical opinions wound up with this sentence, and I had turned back to look at the lithographed sketch of the authoress which fronted the first page of the album, when the fair original re-entered and I laid down the volume on its appropriate table.

'Well, what do you think of them?' said Vorticella, with an emphasis which had some significance unperceived by me. 'I know you are a great student. Give me *your* opinion of these opinions.'

'They must be very gratifying to you,' I answered with a little confusion, for I perceived that I might easily mistake my footing, and I began to have a presentiment of an examination for which I was by no means crammed.

'On the whole – yes,' said Vorticella, in a tone of concession. 'A few of the notices are written with some pains, but not one of them has really grappled with the chief idea in the appendix. I don't know whether you have studied political economy, but you saw what I said on page 398 about the Jersey fisheries?'

I bowed – I confess it – with the mean hope that this movement in the nape of my neck would be taken as sufficient proof that I had read, marked and learned. I do not forgive myself for this pantomimic falsehood, but I was young and morally timorous, and Vorticella's personality had an effect on me something like that of a powerful mesmeriser when he directs all his ten fingers towards your eyes, as unpleasantly visible ducts for the invisible stream. I felt a great power of contempt in her, if I did not come up to her expectations.

'Well,' she resumed, 'you observe that not one of them has taken up that argument. But I hope I convinced you about the dragnets?'

Here was a judgement on me. Orientally speaking, I had lifted up my foot on the steep descent of falsity and was compelled to set it down on a lower level. 'I should think you must be right,' said I, inwardly resolving that on the next topic I would tell the truth.

'I *know* that I am right,' said Vorticella. 'The fact is that no critic in this town is fit to meddle with such subjects, unless it be Volvox, and he, with all his command of language, is very superficial. It is Volvox who writes in the *Monitor* – I hope you noticed how he contradicts himself?'

My resolution, helped by the equivalence of dangers, stoutly prevailed, and I said, 'No.'

'No! I am surprised. He is the only one who finds fault with me. He is a Dissenter, you know. The *Monitor* is the Dissenters' organ, but my husband has been so useful to them in municipal affairs that they would not venture to run my book down; they feel obliged to tell the truth about me. Still, Volvox betrays himself. After praising me for my penetration and accuracy, he presently says I have allowed myself to be imposed upon and have let my active imagination run away with me. That is like his dissenting impertinence. Active my imagination may be, but I have it under control. Little Vibrio, who writes the playful notice in the *Medley Pie*, has a clever hit at Volvox in that passage about the steeplechase of imagination, where the loser wants to make it appear that the winner was only run away with. But if you did not notice Volvox's self-contradiction you would not see the point,' added Vorticella, with rather a chilling intonation. 'Or perhaps you did not read the *Medley Pie* notice? That is a pity. Do take up the book again. Vibrio is a poor little tippling creature, but, as Mr Carlyle would say, he has an eye, and he is always lively.'

I did take up the book again, and read as demanded.

'It is very ingenious,' said I, really appreciating the difficulty of being lively in this connection: it seemed even more wonderful than that a Vibrio should have an eye.

'You are probably surprised to see no notices from the London press,' said Vorticella. 'I have one – a very remarkable one. But I reserve it until the others have spoken, and then I shall introduce it to wind up. I shall have them reprinted, of course, and inserted in future copies. This from the *Candelabrum* is only eight lines in length, but full of venom. It calls my style dull and pompous. I think that will tell its own tale, placed after the other critiques.'

'People's impressions are so different,' said I. 'Some persons find *Don Quixote* dull.'

'Yes,' said Vorticella, in emphatic chest tones, 'dullness is a matter of opinion – but pompous! That I never was and never could be. Perhaps he means that my matter is too important for his taste; and I have no objection to *that*. I did not intend to be trivial. I should just like to read you that passage about the dragnets, because I could make it clearer to you.'

A second (less ornamental) copy was at her elbow and was already opened, when to my great relief another guest was announced, and I was able to take my leave without seeming to run away from *The Channel Islands*, though not without being compelled to carry with me the loan of 'the marked copy', which I was to find advantageous in a re-perusal of the appendix, and was only requested to return before my departure from Pumpiter. Looking into the volume now with some curiosity, I found it a very ordinary combination of the commonplace and ambitious, one of those books which one might imagine to have been written under the old Grub Street* coercion of hunger and thirst, if they were not known beforehand to be the gratuitous productions of ladies and gentlemen whose circumstances might be called altogether easy, but for an uneasy vanity that happened to have been directed towards authorship. Its importance was that of a polypus, tumour, fungus or other erratic outgrowth, noxious and disfiguring in its effect on the individual organism which nourishes it. Poor Vorticella might not have been more wearisome on a visit than the majority of her neighbours, but for this disease of magnified self-importance belonging to small authorship. I understand that the chronic complaint of *The Channel Islands* never left her. As the years went on and the publication tended to vanish in the distance for her neighbours' memory, she was still bent on dragging it to the foreground, and her chief interest in new acquaintances was the possibility of lending them her book, entering into all details concerning it and requesting them to read her album of 'critical opinions'. This really made her more tiresome than Gregarina, whose distinction was that she had had cholera, and who did not feel herself in her true position with strangers until they knew it.

My experience with Vorticella led me for a time into the false supposition that this sort of fungous disfiguration, which makes Self disagreeably larger, was most common to the female sex; but I presently found that here too the male could assert his superiority and show a more vigorous boredom. I have known a man with a single pamphlet containing an assurance that somebody else was wrong, together with a few approved quotations, produce a more powerful effect of shuddering at his approach than ever Vorticella did with her varied octavo volume, including notes and appendix. Males of more than one nation recur to my memory who produced from their pocket on the slightest encouragement a small pink or buff duodecimo pamphlet, wrapped in silver paper, as a present held ready for an intelligent reader. 'A mode of propagandism,' you remark in excuse; 'they wished to spread some useful corrective doctrine.' Not necessarily: the indoctrination aimed at was perhaps to convince you of their own talents by the sample of an 'Ode on Shakespeare's Birthday',* or a translation from Horace.

Vorticella may pair off with Monas, who had also written his one book – *Here and There; or, a Trip from Truro to Transylvania* – and not only carried it in his portmanteau when he went on visits, but took the earliest opportunity of depositing it in the drawing room, and afterwards would enter to look for it, as if under pressure of a need for reference, begging the lady of the house to tell him whether she had seen 'a small volume bound in red'. One hostess at last ordered it to be carried into his bedroom to save his time; but it presently reappeared in his hands, and was again left with inserted slips of paper on the drawing-room table.

Depend upon it, vanity is human, native alike to men and women; only in the male it is of denser texture, less volatile, so that it less immediately informs you of its presence, but is more massive and capable of knocking you down if you come into collision with it; while in women vanity lays by its small revenges as in a needle case always at hand. The difference is in muscle and fingertips, in traditional habits and mental perspective, rather than in the original appetite of vanity. It is an approved method now to explain ourselves by a reference to the races as little like us as possible, which leads me to observe that in Fiji the men use the most elaborate hairdressing, and that wherever tattooing is in vogue the male expects to carry off the prize of admiration for pattern and workmanship. Arguing analogically, and looking for this tendency of the Fijian or Hawaiian male in the eminent European, we must suppose that it exhibits itself under the forms of civilised apparel; and it would be a great mistake to estimate passionate effort by the effect it produces on our perception or understanding. It is conceivable that a man may have concentrated no less will and expectation on his wristbands, gaiters and the shape of his hat brim, or an appearance which impresses you as that of the modern 'swell', than the Ojibwe on an ornamentation which seems to us much more elaborate. In what concerns the search for admiration at least, it is not true that the effect is equal to the cause and resembles it. The cause of a flat curl on the masculine forehead, such as might be seen when George the Fourth was king,* must have been widely different in quality and intensity from the impression made by that small scroll of hair on the organ of the beholder. Merely to maintain an attitude and gait which I notice in certain clubmen, and especially an inflation of the chest accompanying very small remarks, there goes, I am convinced, an expenditure of psychical energy little appreciated by the multitude – a mental vision of Self and deeply impressed beholders which is quite without antitype in what we call the effect produced by that hidden process.

No! There is no need to admit that women would carry away the prize of vanity in a competition where differences of custom were fairly considered. A man cannot show his vanity in a tight skirt which forces him to walk sideways down the staircase; but let the match be between the respective vanities of largest beard and tightest skirt, and here too the battle would be to the strong.

NOTES

'Silly Novels by Lady Novelists' was first published in the *Westminster Review* in 1856; 'Woman in France' was first published in the *Westminster Review* in 1854; 'The Grammar of Ornament' was first published in the *Fortnightly Review* in 1865; 'The Too-Ready Writer' and 'Diseases of Small Authorship' were first published in *Impressions of Theophrastus Such* (a volume of literary essays by an imaginary eccentric scholar – see first note to p. 47) in 1879. The text of this edition is based on that of the first publication, accepting spelling corrections Eliot made in later editions. In some instances, spelling, punctuation and grammar have been silently corrected to make the text more appealing to the modern reader. Italics for emphasis are Eliot's own; in some cases, words rendered in italics as per the convention for foreign language have now entered common usage in English, and therefore are candidates for being rendered in roman; however, given Eliot's penchant for italicising for emphasis, these have been left in italics to preserve the original reading experience.

5   *mauvais moments*: That is, tough times.
6   *Compensation… story of real life*: This refers to *Compensation: A Story of Real Life Thirty Years Ago* (1856) by Georgiana, Lady Chatterton (1806–76).
6   *Ossianic*: Epic, heroic; after the legendary Irish bard.

- 7 *Agape*: From the ancient Greek; the highest form of love, such as the love of God.
- 8 *Creuzer*: Here Eliot invokes Georg Friedrich Creuzer (1771–1858), a German philologist.
- 8 *understand... what is writ about it*: Alexander Pope (1688–1744) on philosopher Henry St John, Viscount Bolingbroke (1678–1751).
- 8 *Laura Gay*: An 1856 two-volume novel (anonymous).
- 8 *dear old ... pleasant Livy*: Roman writers and poets Virgil (Publius Vergilius Maro, 70–19 BC), Horace (Quintus Horatius Flaccus, 65–8 BC), Cicero (Marcus Tullius Cicero, 106–43 BC) and Livy (Titus Livius, 59 BC–AD 17).
- 10 *depôt*: Deposit.
- 10 *lionne*: Lioness.
- 10 *Almack's*: The name of several famous London clubs.
- 10 *Mr Rogers's breakfasts*: At the time breakfast parties were in vogue; the Mr Rogers in question is Samuel Rogers (1763–1855), an English poet, whose breakfasts welcomed eminent literary figures.
- 11 *comme il faut*: Proper.
- 11 *Rank and Beauty*: Another anonymously authored novel published in 1856.
- 11 *Spring Gardens*: A street in St James's, London.
- 11 *objet aimé*: The object of her affection.
- 12 *Vandyke*: That is, like a model for a painting by Sir Anthony Van Dyck (1599–1641), who was known for his portraits of English courtiers.
- 14 *upas tree*: A tree that slowly poisons those around it.
- 14 *It is a fact... bad example*: A quotation from *Woman's Devotion: A Novel* (1855) by Julia Cecilia Stretton (1812–78), from which the following quotations are also taken.

NOTES

14 très vrai: Very true.

15 noumenon: From the philosophy of Immanuel Kant (1724–1804), meaning 'the thing as it is in itself'.

16 Puseyites: Followers of Edward Bouverie Pusey (1800–82), English theologian and founder of the Oxford Movement.

17 The Enigma… Wolchorley House: Another anonymously authored novel, also published in 1856.

18 Loiauté: Loyalty.

19 Dr Cumming… Dr Pusey: John Cumming (1807–81) was a Scottish clergyman and author, and the subject of a critical essay by Eliot, 'Evangelical Teaching: Dr Cumming' (1855); Robert Owen (1771–1858) was a Welsh textile manufacturer and social reformer, who Eliot wrote of in the same essay; for Pusey see note to p. 16.

19 spirit-rappers: That is, those who purport to be able to communicate with spirits via knocking sounds.

19 manches à la chinoise: Chinese-style sleeves, a trend in dressmaking.

22 Pleaceman X: A reference to 'The Three Christmas Waits' by William Makepeace Thackeray (1811–63): 'My name is Pleaceman X;/Last night I was in bed,/A dream did me perplex,/Which came into my Edd…'

25 May Meetings: This is a reference to the meetings held at Exeter Hall (on the Strand, London), which hosted various religious and philanthropic societies, including the British and Foreign Bible Society, the Protestant Reformation Society, the Protestant Association, the Trinitarian Bible Society and the Peace Society.

26 Church of the United Brethren: A protestant Church with roots in America.

26 *Orlando*: A paramour in Shakespeare's *As You Like It*.
27 *The Old Grey Church*: An 1856 novel by Caroline Lucy Scott, Lady Scott (1784–1857), English novelist and religious writer.
27 *Mrs Stowe's pictures… Negroes*: The Mrs Stowe in question is, of course, Harriet Beecher Stowe (1811–96), with whom Eliot corresponded and greatly respected. Given the timing of this essay, Eliot perhaps refers not to Stowe's best-known novel, *Uncle Tom's Cabin* (1852), but to the two-volume novel *Dred: A Tale of the Great Dismal Swamp* (1856). It should be noted that while the language used is considered offensive today, the term was widely used at the time, and no slight is inferred.
28 *Miss Squeers*: This is a reference to a rather pathetic character in Charles Dickens's *Nicholas Nickleby* (1838–39).
29 *Jannes and Jambres… Demetrius the silversmith*: Characters historical and Biblical – for Jannes and Jambres see 2 Timothy 3; for Sennacherib (King of Assyria 705–681, d. 681 BC) see 2 Kings 18–19; for Demetrius see Acts 19.
30 *Was ihr… bespiegeln*: These lines are quoted from *Faust* (1808–32) by Johann Wolfgang von Goethe (1749–1832), which translate to something like, 'What you call the spirit of the ages,/Is but the spirit of humankind,/A mirror in which the times are reflected.'
30 *Adonijah: A Tale of the Jewish Dispersion*: An 1856 novel by Jane Margaret Strickland (1800–88).
31 *Miss Sinclair*: This refers to the Scottish novelist Catherine Sinclair (1800–64).
31 *Dr Daubeny, Mr Mill or Mr Maurice*: That is, eminent learned men: Charles Giles Bridle Daubeny (1795–1867) was a chemist, botanist and geologist; John Stuart Mill

(1806–73) was a philosopher and political economist; and John Frederick Denison Maurice (1805–72) was a theologian and writer.

32 *Harriet Martineau, Currer Bell and Mrs Gaskell*: Harriet Martineau (1802–76) was a social theorist; Currer Bell was the nom de plume of the novelist Charlotte Brontë (1816–55); and Mrs Gaskell is the writer Elizabeth Gaskell (1810–65).

34 *In all labour there is profit*: A quotation from Proverbs 14:23.

35 *La Fontaine's ass*: Jean de La Fontaine (1621–95) was a fabulist; the particular story referred to is obscure.

35 *Moi aussi, je joue de la flute*: 'Me too – I can play the flute.'

37 *Madame de Sablé*: Madeleine de Souvré, marquise de Sablé (1599–1678) was a philosopher, writer and salonnière. Eliot's essay was initially conceived as a book review of an 1854 biography of Sablé by Victor Cousin (1792–1867).

37 *the proportion... deliver to the flames*: A reference to Pedro Perez in *Don Quixote*, who orders Quixote's books be burned to try to cure him of his delusions.

37 *Richardson's Lady G*: That is, Charlotte Grandison, a character in the novel *Sir Charles Grandison* (1753–54) by Samuel Richardson (1689–1761).

40 *Madame de Sévigné*: Marie de Rabutin-Chantal, marquise de Sévigné (1626–96) was an aristocrat and woman of letters.

40 *Madame Dacier*: Anne Le Fèvre Dacier (1647–1720) was a scholar, translator and editor who produced notable translations of the *Iliad* and the *Odyssey*.

40 *Madame Dacier... without shame*: Queen Christina, when Mme Dacier (then Mlle Le Fèvre) sent her a copy of

her edition of *Callimachus*, wrote in reply: '*Mais vous, de qui on m'assure que vous êtes une belle et agréable fille, n'avez vous pas honte d'être si savante?*' (ELIOT'S NOTE.) Loosely translated, this reads: 'But you, whom I am assured are a beautiful and agreeable girl, aren't you ashamed of being so learned?'

40 *Madame de Staël's*: Anne Louise Germaine de Staël-Holstein (1766–1817) was a woman of letters and political theorist.

40 *Madame Roland*: Marie-Jeanne Roland de la Platière (1754–93) was a salonnière and writer.

40 *George Sand*: George Sand was the nom de plume of Amantine Lucile Aurore Dupin de Francueil (1804–76), a novelist, memoirist and journalist.

40 *Jean-Jacques's*: That is, the philosopher, writer and composer Jean-Jacques Rousseau (1712–78).

42 *die of a rose*: A reference to Alexander Pope's *Essay on Man* (Epistle I): 'Or quick effluvia darting thro' the brain,/Die of a rose in aromatic pain'.

43 *marriage de convenance*: Marriage of convenience.

43 *Reunions*: Meetings.

43 *vers de société*: Poetry that covers topical subjects, often light and humorous.

43 *Descartes*: The philosopher René Descartes (1596–1650).

43 *Richelieu*: Armand Jean du Plessis, Duke of Richelieu (1585–1642), a clergyman, was Chief Minister to King Louis XIII.

43 *Hôtel de Rambouillet… 1630*: The Hôtel de Rambouillet was the Paris residence of Catherine de Vivonne, marquise de Rambouillet (1588–1665), who held a renowned salon from 1620–48.

NOTES

43 *the troubles of the Fronde*: The Fronde was a series of civil wars in France (1648–53), during which the aristocracy rebelled against Jules Mazarin (1602–61), Chief Minister of France from 1642, and Louis XIV.

43 *habitués*: Regulars.

44 *Richelieu… and Bossuet*: As Eliot goes on to elaborate, these are famous regulars of the salon at the Hôtel de Rambouillet: for Richelieu see fifth note to p. 43; Pierre Corneille (1606–84) was a playwright; Louis de Bourbon, Prince of Condé (1621–86) was a general; Jean-Louis Guez de Balzac (1597–1654) was an author; and Jacques-Bénigne Lignel Bossuet (1627–1704) was a bishop and theologian.

45 *hommes d'affaires*: Businessmen.

45 *bas bleus*: Bluestockings.

45 *précieux*: Precious.

45 *Précieuses Ridicules… 1673*: Two works by leading playwright, actor and poet Molière (1622–73), which premiered in 1659 and 1672 respectively (Eliot seems to have the dates slightly wrong).

45 *Magdelon and Cathos… Mademoiselle Scudéry*: Magdelon and Cathos are characters from the *Précieuses Ridicules* (see previous note); Madeleine de Scudéry (1607–1701) was a writer associated with the Hôtel de Rambouillet.

45 *bouts-rimés*: Rhyming ends.

45 *Mademoiselle d'Orleans… share in the Fronde*: Anne Marie Louise d'Orléans, Duchess of Montpensier (1627–93) was involved in the rising against Louis XIV, and was exiled from court until 1657.

46 *Madame de Sévigné… La Rochefoucauld*: For Madame de Sévigné see first note to p. 40; Marie-Madeleine

Pioche de La Vergne, Comtesse de La Fayette (1634–93) was a novelist marked for her historical fiction; François, Duc de La Rochefoucauld (1613–80) was a moralist.

46 *M. Cousin*: See first note to p. 37.

46 *Ségrais... Divers Portraits*: Jean Regnault de Segrais (1624–1701) was a poet and novelist. He is often considered Madame d'Orléans's assistant, and it is her name on the title page of this volume.

47 *La Bruyère adopted the form in his Characters*: Jean de La Bruyère (1645–96) was a philosopher and moralist. His *Caractères* is a collection of maxims and portraits, modelled after the book of *Characters* by the Greek philosopher Theophrastus ($c.371$–$c.287$ BC) – which, incidentally, also served as the inspiration for Eliot's book of caricatures, *Impressions of Theophrastus Such* (1879).

47 *Athenaeum*: A British literary magazine describing itself as 'a journal of literature, science and the fine arts', published from 1828–1921.

48 *Philosophical Journal*: This is a reference to *The Philosophical Magazine* (at that time known as *The Philosophical Magazine and Journal*).

48 *Madame Geoffrin's... young wife*: Marie Thérèse Rodet Geoffrin (1699–1777) was one of the leading female figures in the French Enlightenment, noted for the salons she ran; Jean-Baptiste le Rond d'Alembert (1717–83) was a mathematician, physicist, philosopher and music theorist; Jeanne Julie Éléonore de Lespinasse (1732–76) was a woman of letters; Friedrich Melchior, Baron von Grimm (1723–1807) was a journalist and art critic; Marie Jean Antoine Nicolas de Caritat, Marquis of Condorcet (Nicolas de Condorcet, 1743–94) was a philosopher and

mathematician; his wife, Sophie de Condorcet (1764–1822), also a philosopher, was a popular society figure.

48 *femme auteur*: Woman author.

48 *Rousseau's horror in Madame d'Epinay*: Louise Florence d'Épinay (1726–83) was a writer and woman of fashion; she had several highly publicised liaisons, including with Baron von Grimm (see above) and Jean-Jacques Rousseau (see final note to p. 40), who later wrote unpleasantly about her in his *Confessions* (1782).

49 *Bossuet and Massillon... Rousseau*: That is, theologians Bossuet (see note to p. 44) and Jean-Baptiste Massillon (1663–1742), Bishop of Clermont from 1717–42, and writers François-Marie Arouet, known by his nom de plume Voltaire (1694–1778) and Jean-Jacques Rousseau (see final note to p. 40).

49 *a volume... Duchess de Longueville*: Cousin wrote several volumes on Anne-Geneviève de Bourbon, the Duchess of Longueville (1619–79); Eliot refers here to *La jeunesse de Mme de Longueville* (1853).

49 *Conrart*: Valentin Conrart (1603–75) was an author, and a founder of the Académie française.

49 *Valant*: Nothing is known of Dr Valant beyond the details given in Eliot's description.

50 *un heureux... et de bonté*: A happy mixture of reason, wit, pleasure and kindness.

50 *tons criards*: Garish tones.

50 *Marquis of Courtenvaux*: Gilles de Souvré, Marquis de Courtanvaux, Baron de Lezines (*c.*1540–1626) was entrusted with the education of the dauphin, Louis XIII.

51 *Madame de Motteville*: Françoise Bertaut de Motteville (*c.*1621–89) was a memoirist.

51 *beaucoup de lumière et de sincérité*: Much light and sincerity.
51 *Catherine de Medici*: Catherine de' Medici (1519–89) was an Italian noblewoman; the wife of Henry II (1519–59, r. 1547–59), she was Queen of France from 1547–59.
51 *finezas*: Refined, courteous people (literally, 'refined' in the plural).
52 *femme précieuse*: Precious woman.
52 *Duc de Montmorency*: Henri II de Montmorency (1595–1632) was a nobleman and military commander.
52 *Tallemant de Réaux*: Gédéon Tallemant, Sieur des Réaux (1619–92) was a writer known for his *Historiettes* (1834), short, often scandalous biographies.
52 *Mademoiselle Dona d'Attichy… Maure*: Anne Maure (1600–63).
52 *Julie de Rambouillet… Montausier*: Julie d'Angennes, Duchess of Montausier (1607–71).
53 *lèse-amitié*: That is, the crime of killing a friendship
53 *galimatias*: 'Rigmarole', i.e. going through the motions.
54 *these lines of Bertaut… savoir*: Ignorance is unfortunate/ And knowledge even more so. Jean Bertaut (1552–1611) was a court poet.
55 *Sainte-Beuve… Madame Necker*: Charles Augustin Sainte-Beuve (1804–69) was a literary critic; Suzanne Curchod (1737–94) was a writer, known for hosting one of the most celebrated salons of the time. (She was married to the finance minister, Jacques Necker (1732–1804), hence 'Madame Necker'.)
56 *Mlle de Chalais… the Marquise*: That is, lady in waiting to de Sablé. (Nothing is known of de Chalais.)
57 *M. Chaudebonne*: Claude d'Urre, Lord of Chaudebonne (1577–1644) of the Swiss Guard was said by Tallemant

NOTES

(see third note to p. 52) to be Madame de Rambouillet's best friend.

- 57 *Voiture*: Vincent Voiture (1597–1648) was a poet and writer.
- 58 *Princesse de Paphlagonia*: That is, *Relation de l'Isle Imaginaire: Histoire de la Princesse de Paphlagonie* (1659).
- 58 *Hippocrates and Galen*: Greek physicians, Hippocrates (*c*.460–377 BC) and Aelius Galenus (AD 129–99).
- 59 *Port-Royalists*: Port-Royal-des-Champs was a Cistercian abbey in Magny-les-Hameaux, south-west of Paris. The inhabitants were adherents to Jansenism (a Catholic movement started by Cornelius Jansen (1585–1638), later declared heretical). The order was dedicated to study, and attracted significant figures through its doors.
- 59 *En verité… me saigner?*: 'In truth, I believe I could not do better than to leave everything and go there. But what would become of these fears of having no physicians to choose from, nor a surgeon to bleed me?'
- 59 *Friandise*: Treats.
- 60 *bonnes bouches*: Sweet treats usually eaten after a meal.
- 60 *Je vous demande… j'en ai scrupule*: 'I ask you, in the name of God, that you do not cook me any rich foods. Above all, don't give me a feast. In the name of God, let there be nothing more than can be eaten, for you know it is of no use to me; moreover, I have qualms about it.'
- 62 *Scarron… dames perle très fine*: 'The unparalleled Bois-Dauphine, Between ladies the pearl most fine.' Paul Scarron (1610–60) was a poet, dramatist and novelist.
- 62 *Réné de Longueil, Seigneur de Maisons*: René de Longueil, (later) Marquis de Maisons (1596–1677) was Surintendant des Finances under Louis XIV.

62 *blockade of Paris in 1649*: Part of the Fronde (see penultimate note to p. 43).

62 *Condé*: See note to p. 44.

62 *Chancellor Séguier's*: Pierre Séguier (1588–1672) was a statesman, and was Chancellor from 1635.

62 *Lenet... Gourville*: Pierre Lenet (d. 1671) was a prosecutor, attached to the house of Condé, and became Councillor of State in *c.*1645. Jean Hérault, Baron of Gourville (1625–1703) was an adventurer and aristocrat.

63 *lustrum*: A period of five years – i.e. approaching 60.

63 *Puseyism*: See note to p. 16.

63 *récherché*: Studious.

64 *vaquer enfin... sa santé*: That is, she could 'finally go about at ease, with every care for her salvation and her health'.

64 *whom Pascal sought... replis da cœur*: The Pascal is question is Blaise Pascal (1623–62), a mathematician, physicist and philosopher. Antoine Arnauld (1612–94) was a theologian, philosopher and mathematician, and was one of the more notable members of Port-Royal. His *Port-Royal Logic* (*La logique, ou l'art de penser*), a textbook on logic, was published in 1662. The quote attributed to La Rochefoucauld here is a little confused, but is taken to mean something like, 'You know I believe only you are to be trusted with certain chapters, and especially with matters of secrets of the heart.'

65 *It is into her ear... La Rochefoucauld*: The letter to which we allude has this charming little touch: '*Je hais comme la mort que les gens de son age puissent croire que j'ai des galanteries. Il semble qu'on leur parait cent ans des qu'on est plus vieille qu'eux, et ils sont tout propre à s'étonner qu'il y ait encore question des gens.*' (ELIOT'S NOTE.) That is, something along the lines of,

'I hate like death that people of his age should believe that I have liaisons. It seems one is perceived to be a hundred years old to those you are older than, and they are all too often astonished that there are still any men around one.'

66 *Je crois… Madame, votre, etc.*: 'I believe only I can manage to do the exact opposite of what I want to do, because it is true that there is no one I wish to honour more than you, and I have acted so that it is almost impossible for you to believe it. My failure to write to you for such a very long time was not enough to persuade you that I am unworthy of your good graces and of your memory — I had to delay another fortnight before having the honour of answering your letter. In truth, madam, it makes me appear so guilty that towards anyone other than you I would rather be held accountable than undertake such a difficult thing as that of justifying myself. But I feel so innocent in my soul, and I have so much esteem, respect and affection for you, that it seems to me that you must know it from a hundred leagues away, even though I haven't said a word. This is what gives me the courage to write to you at this hour, but it is not what has kept me from doing so for so long. At first my failure was due to suffering a lot of pain, and since then I have done so out of shame, and I confess to you that if it wasn't for the confidence and reassurance you give me, and that which I derive from my own feelings for you, I would never dare to undertake to remind you of me; but I assure myself that you will forget all my faults upon the protest I make to you and my assurance that I shall not let myself be hardened in them faults again, and to remain inviolably, madam, yours, etc.'

- 66 *Madame de Hautefort... Domat*: Marie de Hautefort (1616–91) was a noblewoman and favourite of Louis XIII; Pierre Nicole (1625–95) was a theologian, writer and moralist, and one of the foremost figures of the Jansenists; Jean Domat (1625–96) was a jurist and close friend of Port-Royalists.
- 66 *Rohault invented his glass tubes*: Jacques Rohault (1618–72) was a philosopher, physicist and mathematician (and follower of Cartesianism); his 'glass tubes' were part of a barometric design that demonstrated capillary action.
- 67 *the best Pensées... La Rochefoucauld*: Blaise Pascal's *Pensées* (*Thoughts*) were first published after his death in 1670; La Rochefoucauld's *Maxims* were first published in 1665.
- 67 *M. d'Andilly*: Robert Arnauld d'Andilly (1589–1674), who lived at Port-Royal-des-Champs, was a Councillor of State.
- 68 *horibile dictu!*: A horrible saying!
- 68 *L'envie de faire des maximes se gagne comme la rhume*: 'The urge to make maxims is caught like the common cold.'
- 68 *Jacques Esprit*: Jacques Esprit (1611–77) was a moralist and writer.
- 68 *La Faussete des vertus humaines*: Literally, *The Fallacy of Human Virtues*, this was published (in two volumes) only after his death (1678–1709).
- 69 *Voilà tout... ragoût de mouton*: 'These are all the maxims I have; but I don't give nothing for nothing, so I ask you for a carrot soup, a mutton stew...'
- 70 *On ne pourroit faire... mon libérateur*: 'One could not make an instruction more proper to convert a catechumen, spirit and will, to God... If there were only this writing and the Gospel in the world, I would be a Christian. One

would teach me to recognise my miseries, the other to beseech my deliverer for release.'

70 *Madame de Maintenon*: Françoise d'Aubigné (1635–1719) was a noblewoman and wife of Louis XIV.

70 *Madame de Schomberg*: That is, Marie de Hautefort (see second note to p. 66).

70 *those who observed the rule of Helvetius*: Here Eliot invokes the later writer Claude Adrien Helvétius (1715–71), whose 1758 treatise *De l'esprit* (*On the Mind*) claimed all human faculties are attributes of physical sensation, and that the only real motive is self-interest, and therefore there is no good or evil.

71 *Journal des savants*: Originally the *Journal des sçavans*, the journal was established in 1665, and is considered the earliest European academic journal.

71 *Je vous envoie… de ce dictum*: 'I am sending you what I was able to extract from my mind to put in the *Journal des savants*. I have put in that part which you feel so strongly about, so that you can overcome the shame which made you send the preface without cutting anything out; and I was not afraid to include it, because I am sure that you won't have it printed, even if you like the rest. I also assure you that I will be no more obliged to you if you use it than if you correct it or throw it into the fire. We great authors are too rich to fear losing any small part of our productions. Tell me what you think of this dictum.'

72 *Sacy… Duc de Luynes*: Sacy and Le Maître are possibly the same person – Louis-Isaac Lemaistre de Sacy (1613–1684), a priest of Port-Royal and renowned theologian; for Arnauld and Nicole see second note to p. 64 and second note to p. 66 respectively; Louis-Charles

d'Albert de Luynes (1620–90) was a translator and moralist. This translation, known as the Bible de Port-Royal, was the most widespread Bible edition in France in the eighteenth century.

76 *during the reigns… two Charleses*: That is, from 1603–85.

77 *The Grammar of Ornament*: This essay is in response to the 1856 publication of the design sourcebook *The Grammar of Ornament* by British architect Owen Jones (1809–74).

77 *Teufelsdröckh*: A reference to the titular character of *Sartor Resartus: The Life and Opinions of Herr Teufelsdröckh* (1831) by Thomas Carlyle (1795–1881), a mock-commentary on the life of a fictional German philosopher, Diogenes Teufelsdröckh (a name which translates as, 'God-born Devil's dung').

83 *Isidore of Seville or a Vincent of Beauvais*: Isidore of Seville (*c*.560–636) was a scholar and theologian; Vincent of Beauvais (*c*.1190–*c*.1264) was a Dominican friar and scholar at Royaumont Abbey.

83 *gratis anhelans, multa agendo nihil agens*: Loosely, 'Out of breath to no purpose, very busy doing nothing'.

84 *Rasselas*: *The History of Rasselas, Prince of Abissinia* (1759) is a fable about bliss and ignorance by Samuel Johnson (1709–84).

87 *as an ancient Rabbi… untruth is untruth*: This is attributed by scholars to Abtalion, a rabbinic sage in the early pre-Mishnaic era.

88 *Rienzi or Notre Dame de Paris*: Respectively, an 1835 opera by Richard Wagner (1813–83) and the 1831 novel better known in English as *The Hunchback of Notre-Dame* by Victor Hugo (1802–85).

90 *coup d'oeil*: Glance.

NOTES

90   *merry-andrew's dress*: That is, a clown's clothing.

92   *Sadness is a kind of mirth... merry*: From *The Two Noble Kinsmen* (1634), attributed jointly to Shakespeare and John Fletcher (1579–1625).

94   *the author of the Areopagitica*: That is, John Milton (1608–74). In full, this was published as *Areopagitica: A Speech of Mr John Milton for the Liberty of Unlicenc'd Printing, to the Parliament of England* (1644).

98   *Grub Street*: A street in London inhabited by impoverished writers.

99   *'Ode on Shakespeare's Birthday'*: Possibly a reference to an 1864 poem of this name by John Sheppard (1785–1879), a religious writer.

101   *when George the Fourth was king*: That is, 1820–30.

OTHER CLASSIC NON-FICTION FROM RENARD PRESS

ISBN: 9781913724733
224pp • Paperback • £7.99

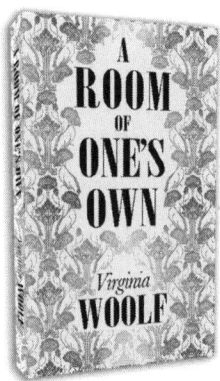

ISBN: 9781913724009
160pp • Paperback • £7.99

ISBN: 9781913724306
60pp • Paperback • £5

ISBN: 9781913724641
160pp • Paperback • £7.99

ISBN: 9781913724047
64pp • Paperback • £6.99

ISBN: 9781913724702
128pp • Paperback • £5.99

DISCOVER THE FULL COLLECTION AT WWW.RENARDPRESS.COM